FELLOWSHIP IN JUDAISM

By the same author:
A LIFE OF RABBAN YOHANAN BEN ZAKKAI
(Leiden, 1962)

FELLOWSHIP IN JUDAISM

THE FIRST CENTURY AND TODAY

JACOB NEUSNER

*Research Associate in Jewish History
Philip W. Lown Institute of Advanced Judaic Studies,
Brandeis University*

With a Preface by
ROBERT A. NISBET
*Dean of the College of Letters and Science,
University of California, Riverside*

LONDON
VALLENTINE · MITCHELL

First Published by
Vallentine, Mitchell & Co. Ltd.,
18 Cursitor Street, London E.C.4

© Jacob Neusner 1963

*Set, printed and bound in Great Britain
by Tonbridge Printers Ltd*

CONTENTS

	page
Preface by Professor Robert A. Nisbet	7
Foreword	9
I. Qumran and Jerusalem: Two Jewish Ways to Fellowship	11
II. Fellowship Through Law: The *Haber*	22
III. Fellowship Through Intellect: The *Talmid Hakham*	31
IV. An After-word: Jewish Fellowship Today	60
Index	75

Footnotes and references will be found at the end of each chapter

TO MY MOTHER
Psalm 92.6

PREFACE

I judge there to be at least three ways of appreciating this excellent book. First, and most obviously, it is a study in religious history. What Dr. Neusner has to say about the role of the religious fellowship in first-century Pharisaic Judaism is fruitful and clarifying to those primarily interested in the history of Judaism. Resting on the primary sources and steeped in the scholarship of the subject, Dr. Neusner's book is a valuable addition to the literature of religious history.

But the book is more than religious history. It is a perceptive essay in religious sociology, one that falls in the great tradition of such men as Max Weber and Troeltsch. The detailed analysis we are given of the two varieties of religious fellowship is as instructive to those concerned with the problem of community and association as it is to religious historians. It would be hard to improve upon Dr. Neusner's sociological treatment of the voluntary association—its conditions of rise and survival, and its relation to the surrounding moral and institutional order.

Finally, the book should be regarded as a profound essay in meaning for our own time. To follow Dr. Neusner in his portrayal of first-century Judaism is to note at every turn implicit analogy with our own age. We too find ourselves living in what Dr. Neusner calls a crisis of community. Ours is a crisis compounded of many of the same elements that existed in the earlier age—social dislocation, alienation, and the struggle for identity and meaning. And because the crisis today is analogous to that of the first century, few will doubt, I believe, that the role of fellowship has comparable significance in the two ages. As Dr. Neusner is careful to remind us, fellowship will not save the world, nor even probably make a substantial difference to the Jewish community. But to the individual the value of the fellowship is, or can be, not inconsiderable. I like Dr. Neusner's concluding words. 'If it has any value at all the fellowship must be regarded as a tentative and austere step towards meaningful and creative use of that interim between birth and death that each man knows as life.'

ROBERT A. NISBET

FOREWORD

THE ESSAYS THAT follow attempt to elucidate two varieties of religious fellowship in first-century Pharisaic Judaism, the first created by Pharisaic emphasis on certain neglected details of Jewish law; the second, by Pharisaic emphasis on study of the Torah. I have limited my discussion to the evidence relevant to the later decades of the Second Jewish Commonwealth, because the characteristics of these groups before the destruction of Jerusalem in 70 C.E. may be relatively clearly discerned, while it is difficult to ascertain changes in their nature after the destruction of Jerusalem in 70 C.E., on the one hand, or, on the other, to discover precisely what social groups were produced by Pharisaism in its earlier period.

Though originally printed separately, these papers were part of a single line of inquiry, and were intended to form a continuous discussion. Therefore I take the liberty of presenting them together here, each essay being somewhat altered from its original form. I have, moreover, included discussion of the implications of first-century Jewish religious fellowship for contemporary Judaism. Occasionally one's historical studies yield information relevant to his own day. Since I believe it to be the case in this instance, I have attempted to suggest the applicability of some of the information from the earlier age, without, hopefully, prejudicing the case for the results of my more detached historical inquiry.

The papers were originally published as follows: 'Qumran and Jerusalem, Two Jewish Roads to Utopia,' *Journal of Bible and Religion*, 1959 pp. 284-290; 'The Fellowship [Haburah] in the Second Jewish Commonwealth,' *Harvard Theological Review* LIII, 1960, pp. 125-142; 'Father of

Wisdom,' from *A Life of Rabban Yohanan ben Zakkai* (Leiden, 1962), and, for the epilogue, 'Fellowship and the Crisis of Community' and 'Five Principles of Fellowship,' *The Reconstructionist*, XXVI, 19, pp. 8-16, and XXVII, 11, pp. 21-24.

These essays are published with the help of generous grants from The Alexander Kohut Memorial Foundation in New York City and the Board of Rabbis of Greater Philadelphia. I am grateful for this support.

My thanks are due also to Professor Robert A. Nisbet for his interest in my studies, and for his willingness to introduce them.

JACOB NEUSNER.

Waltham, Massachusetts
Erev Rosh Hodesh Shevat, 5723
January 25, 1963.

I

QUMRAN AND JERUSALEM

Two Jewish Ways to Fellowship

THE MODERN WORLD knows two forms of Utopianism, social and revolutionary. The social Utopian would restore society to its ancient ideal, proposing to reconstruct the city out of its own stone and mortar. The revolutionary Utopian would build a new society on the ruins of the old, destroying in order to create. These two Utopian forms recall the efforts of 'moral men' in an earlier 'immoral society,' that of Jewish Palestine during the Second Commonwealth. In the centuries before the start of the Christian Era, these men drew apart from the common life to discover social forms capable of embodying religious ideals.

The central issue of the Jewish Commonwealth was how to transform biblical precept into daily practice. It was, therefore, religious rather than humanitarian Utopianism that moved men to dream of a better world: how to translate the vision of lawgiver and prophet into the workaday situation of a later and lesser age. Biblical Judaism had taught that the pious man ought to love those who love God, and to abhor those who despise Him. 'Blessed is the man who walks not in the counsel of the wicked, nor stands in the way of sinners, nor sits in the seat of scoffers . . .' (Psalm 1:1). Conversely the pious man says, 'I am a companion of all who fear Thee and of those who keep Thy precepts' (Psalm 119:63). The Psalmist's choice of the word COMPANION (*haber*) connotes more than merely FRIEND, but rather FELLOW-WORSHIPPER, one who is an associate in a common sacred task. Indeed the word recalls an earlier pagan and Pre-Mosaic meaning, to tie together by magic charm, knot, or spell. In the Second Commonwealth there were many such 'charmed circles,' groups of companions who came together to form fellowships of the faithful. These communes took two forms. That founded at Qumran represented revolutionary Utopianism, and those founded in Jerusalem and elsewhere social Utopianism. This paradigm may offer some insight into the sociology of Judaism at a crucial moment in Jewish history.

The wilderness communes were drawn by the vision of the wilderness, the setting for Israel's holiest drama, and recalled the compelling words of Jeremiah 'I remember the devotion of your youth, your love as a bride, how you followed me in the wilderness, in an unsown land' (Jeremiah 2:2). In the sun-parched hills, the members of the commune thought to make a new beginning, to create a sanctuary of purity in the land they thought to be profaned. These communes, of which there were many, saw themselves morally secure only behind the barrier of rough terrain and within a high wall of discipline. The Qumran group escaped from sinful men in order to found a better and holier society: 'This is the regulation for the men of the community who devote themselves to turn away from every evil and to hold fast to everything which He has commanded as His pleasure: they shall separate themselves from the assembly of men of deceit, they shall be a community, with Torah study.'[1] The Psalmist of Qumran likewise expressed this attitude:

> The nearer I draw to Thee
> The more I am filled with zeal
> Against all that do wickedness.
> For they that draw near to Thee
> Cannot see Thy commandments defied . . .

So for mine own part, I will admit
No comrade into fellowship with men,
Save by the measure of his understanding . . .

Only as Thou drawest a man unto Thee
Will I draw him unto myself,
And as Thou keepest him afar,
So too will I abhor him.

I will not enter into communion
With them that turn their back upon Thy covenant.[2]

(The members of the wilderness communes whom Philo called Essenes likewise avoided the cities 'because of the iniquities which have become inveterate among city dwellers, for they know that their company would have a deadly effect upon their own souls.'[3]) The wilderness communes brought together very good Jews, fully normative, if somewhat abnormal, in their devotion to the Torah and to both its moral and its ritual precepts.[4] They followed the main lines of Jewish law as meticulously as the men in the synagogues whom they abandoned in their flight. They did indeed have their peculiar emphases, both in theology and in ritual, but this marked them apart as a heterodoxy, not a heresy. The men of Qumran were zealous, too deeply committed to the sacred to believe and behave according to the common faith. Escape to the wilderness provided a way to purer, holier life than the men of the cities promised ever to live.

The alternative was the road to Utopia chosen by some of the Pharisees of Jerusalem. They founded religious communes within the common society of the villages and towns, and lived the holy life among profane and ordinary men. This was the way of the Pharisaic fellowship (called HABURAH), which brought together some of the larger number of Jews who identified themselves with the Pharisaic viewpoint (It is emphasized that not all Pharisees were demonstrably members of the Pharisaic fellowship at any time, although all members of the fellowship were probably

Pharisees, adhering to their interpretation of Judaism.) In the words of Josephus, 'they are able greatly to persuade the body of the people, and whatsoever they do about divine worship . . . they perform according to their direction, insomuch that the cities give great attestations to them on account of their entire virtuous conduct, both in the actions of their lives and their discourses also.'[5] The Pharisaic sages taught their followers, 'Do not separate yourself from the community,'[6] but on the contrary, they lived among the masses, teaching and admonishing, seeking to bring all men closer to their Father in heaven. They sought out the heart of the people, and were willing, according to the Gospel, to 'traverse sea and land to make a single proselyte' (Matt. 23:15). Thus they exercised formidable influence over the mind of Jewish Palestine.

At the same time, however, the Pharisaic fellows distinguished themselves from the common people by observing even the most neglected details of the Torah, the laws of ritual purity and by giving tithes and heave offerings as set forth in Scripture. In doing so, they cast up a barrier between themselves and the outsider (called in the sources *Am-Ha-aretz*), for an outsider was for many reasons a potential source of ritual defilement. Even in the towns and villages, therefore, the HABURAH formed a separate society. Two biblical precepts contended in the Pharisaic ethics: first, that all Israel is to be a kingdom of priests and a holy people (and this was understood to mean at the very least a people ritually pure and holy), and second, that every individual Jew everywhere was himself to be as ritually fit as a priest to perform the sacrificial act in the Temple. The Pharisees believed in the sanctity of all Israel, and passionately affirmed the obligation of every Jew to his King. Obsessed with the vision of life and society sanctified in every detail by the commandments of the Torah, they observed and taught the Jewish people to carry out even those laws which were both troublesome and generally ignored.

Although the masses of the people regarded the acts of

careful tithing and ritual purification as far beyond the proper task of a Jew, the fellows were not prepared to give up the struggle. They founded their associations in the villages and towns, among the people but not of them. (These associations were not organizations in the pattern of Qumran, and had neither officers nor formal constitution, but were rather groups of people who recognized one another as part of the same fellowship of observant and pious men.) They taught their eccentricities of observance by example, ever aware not to imitate their students. Thus they sought at once to transform and to transcend society, to 'live Utopia' in an 'unredeemed' world. They elaborated laws to govern the infinite specific situations presented by ritually pure life among defiled men. In such a way the fellows resolved the tension between the precept that demanded sanctification of all Israel, on the one hand, and of every Jew, on the other.

All the communes went far beyond the measure of the Law. Some, and among them the associations described by Philo and Josephus as Essenes, by the Qumran documents as the Many, and by the Zadokite Fragments as the Congregation, thought to find a way to God in the solitude of the wilderness. What sets the Pharisaic fellowship apart is the search for the Godly community within the society of men.

In ancient times the commune was a widespread form of social organization for religion. It was common to the Pythagorean schools of Hellenistic Egypt and to the Nabataean kingdom to the south of the Dead Sea. Jewish Palestine itself provided rich analogues to the Pharisaic order. Many of the sects, particularly the Essenes and the Qumran group, shared with the Pharisees common institutional forms. Indeed Josephus characterizes the social form of Judaism as a series of self-sufficient sects, and the similarities between the Qumran association and the groups known in Josephus and Philo as Essenes and Pharisees have impelled scholars to identify the Qumran literature with one or another known group. The specific forms of the Pharisaic fellowship were determined, however, by the particular obsession of the associates: food.

The Bible had commanded Jews to return to God through the priests and Levites some part of the gifts of the land. Traditions of the time ascribed to Abraham, and later to Saul, the practice of eating even the remaining unconsecrated produce in a state of ritual purity. Tradition likewise ascribed to Solomon the practice of washing hands before a meal as an act of ritual purification. Thus every Jew was obligated to eat his 'secular' (unconsecrated) produce in the purity which characterized the Temple priest in his holy office. This concern was entirely natural in the ancient world, where ritual purity was the common concern of pagan temple, mystery cult, and even of the philosophical schools of the Pythagoreans. In very early days, the Pharisaic fellowship took on specific form and precise definition from the effort to observe the difficult religious obligations of tithing and ritual purity. Even by the first century the schools of Hillel and Shamai disputed certain details in the rule of the fellowship, indicating both a fixed tradition and sufficient interval in which to forget some details. The purpose of the fellowship from the first was to carry out the obligations incumbent on all men.

The Qumran community shared this obsession with ritual defilement, regarding even the Temple as irreparably unclean. They established themselves in the wilderness and elaborated rules by which others might reach their sanctity through a year of probation, a vote of the members, and a second, novitiatory year. The Essenes likewise admitted a newcomer into their fellowship by stages. Josephus records: 'A candidate anxious to join their sect is not immediately admitted. For one year, during which he remains outside the fraternity, they prescribe for him their own rule of life ... Having given proof of his temperance during this probationary period, he is brought into closer touch with the rule, and is allowed to share in the purer kind of holy water, but is not yet received into the meeting of the community ...

After this exhibition of endurance his character is tested for two years more, and only then if found worthy is he enrolled in the society. But before he may touch the common food, he is made to swear tremendous oaths . . .'[7]

The Pharisees received into their fellowship any Jew who undertook to nourish his body in a manner appropriate to the sanctity of his soul. Not all followers of the Pharisees accepted the rule of the fellowship. There were many kinds of Pharisee, as both the Talmud and the Gospels recognize, and there were even sages who were considered outsiders in relationship to the fellowship. A slave might become an associate without his master, and vice versa. The specific rules of affiliation were exhaustive and beyond them there were no distinctions between members and outsiders. The testimony of outsiders was accepted in regard to the KASHRUT (legal fitness) of food, but not in regard to its ritual purity. Thus they were presumed to adhere to the dietary laws, like all good Jews, even though they stood outside the fellowship.[8]

Transcending family, caste, and class distinctions, the fellowship established a new polity within the old society of city and village, a community based upon the willingness of the individual to assume obligations imposed upon him by an ancient and unrepudiated commandment. This disruption in the social order recalls the Gospel saying, 'I have come not to bring peace but a sword . . . For I have come to set a man against his father and a daughter against her mother.' (Matt. 10:34-37). The fellowship represented a considerable complication in the urban order. The city could contend with men who separated themselves from the common life in exclusive alien communes in the wilderness. Reciprocal indifference may have governed the day-to-day contact between the new society at Qumran and the old. Even the Essenes in their villages and neighbourhoods in the towns apparently faced inward towards their commune. On the other hand, the Pharisaic association posed a peculiar problem for the general society. At many intimate and some crucial relationships in daily life, the fellow was guided by a complicated rule that made social intercourse intricate and delicate. The wilderness heterodoxies formed new polities built on the ruins of the old, and the individual moved from one exhaustive clearly defined and exclusive pattern of human relationships into another equally comprehensive and unambiguous situation. The act of the self-conscious, private individual began and ended with the act of affiliation to the new order. For the Pharisaic associate, on the other hand, entry into the new polity was only the first step on a path towards individualism and disintegration of customary social patterns.[9]

A new member of the HABURAH discovered that his relationships with outsiders had become fundamentally transformed. He could no longer associate with any man freely and carelessly. In certain ways his social intercourse completely changed in character, and in every way he had to rearrange his habits of daily life into a new and complex structure.

Obedience to the rule of the order meant that special concern for the sanctity of food entered into hitherto simple social relationships. The implications of the rule were thus translated in very great detail into everyday terms. The rules called for new adjustments in the life of the fellow, multiplying the problems bound up in living with men indifferent to obligations he considered sacred. The obvious solution to these problems was to retreat to neighbourhoods dominated by the commune, or to escape entirely from the common, defiled society. This option was, however, precisely what the fellowship rejected at the start.

The particular emphasis on ritual purity and tithing indicates that the HABURAH was fundamentally a society for strict observance of laws of ritual cleanliness and holy offerings. This was, indeed, all it might have been. Membership in the association could be achieved only through adherence to a pattern of actions which demonstrated devotion to neglected commandments and traditions of

Judaism. In urban society deeds alone truly marked the man, rather than any commitment of faith or intellect. The social relations in the city, brief and random at best, could not manifest any profound virtue of mind or heart. They could, however, serve as a tentative measure of a man's willingness to serve God in ways held particularly significant. The fellowships were open to hypocrites, it is true, and the Gospels and Rabbinic sources give evidence that a faith expressed only through deeds might represent in the end only a meaningless pattern of naked gestures. Such a perplexity troubled the Pharisaic fellows and their heirs.

In the wilderness commune, on the other hand, the total personality of an individual became relevant. 'When he enters into the covenant ... then they shall examine their spiritual qualities in the community, in their mutual relationship, according to everybody's insight and actions ... They shall register them in the order, one before the other, according to his insight and his doings ...'[10] In Qumran the commune examined a man about 'his intelligence and his actions ...' Likewise the Zadokite Community examined newcomers, each 'about his actions and his understanding and his strength and his property ...'[11] In the close life of the wilderness commune, all these things were relevant and important. In the towns and villages only deeds spoke compellingly about a man.

The prosaic literature of Pharisaic law represented, therefore, the comprehensive articulation of all that could ever characterize such a fellowship. Unlike the wilderness associations, the HABURAH could have no other standard but how a man carried out his religious obligations throughout the subtle patterns of daily life. The associates in the intellectual classes, sitting in the academies, schools, and courts of Palestinian Jewry, did in truth reveal the almost unlimited intellectual dimension of their order and its cause. The following story indicates, however, their unrelenting emphasis on the act as the final measure of the man:

Akabya ben Mahaleleel testified to four opinions. His colleagues answered, Akabya, retract these four opinions that thou hast given, and we shall make thee Father of the Court in Israel. He said to them: Better that I be called a fool all my days than that I be made a godless man before God even for an hour; for they shall not say of me, He retracted for the sake of office ... In the hour that he died, he said to his son, My son, retract the four opinions which I gave. His son answered, Why didst not thou retract? He answered, I heard them from a majority, and they also heard their opinions from a majority. I continued steadfast to the tradition that I heard, and so did they. But thou hast heard a decision both from an individual and from the majority. It is better to leave the opinion of the individual and to hold the opinion of the majority. His son answered, Father, commend me to thy fellow sages. He said, I commend thee not. He answered, Perchance thou hast found in me some cause for complaint. Akabya answered, No, but thine own deeds will bring thee near, or thine own deeds will remove thee far [from the fellowship].[12]

The fellows of the academic sages in the streets and fields of the land likewise wove a fabric of actions that represented the effort to build God's kingdom on earth.

The Qumran community chose a revolutionary path to Utopia. The men who fled to the Judean desert abandoned all hope of restoring society or of rebuilding it on its imperfect foundation. At Qumran they established their order, defined its rule, and prepared the way for others to join them. In all this they demonstrated from their city on the hill above the Dead Sea that God was truly sovereign on earth. Their rule was simple, neither elaborated nor complicated by a repudiated past. The men of Qumran struck out to build their new city upon the ruins of the old.

The Pharisaic fellowship made a moral decision to endure the 'iniquities inveterate among city dwellers' so that men far from God's way might return to it through precept and example. The associates consecrated themselves to keep the neglected ordinances governing tithes and ritual purity. They too defined the rule of their order, educated men in the manner of keeping it, and determined a sequence of concerns by which an outsider might come by degrees to enter into fellowship. The infinite implications of the rule for day-to-day affairs were spelled out, and the precise, detailed information so gained made it possible for the associates to keep the faith in the company of men who did not. It was, in fact, law which made possible the Pharisaic choice of a social way to Utopia.

The dilemma of the Pharisaic fellowship, and the manner of its resolution, continue to speak out of the troubling question of Hillel:

> If I am not for myself, then who will be for me?
> But being only for myself, what am I?
> And if not now, when?[13]

NOTES AND REFERENCES

[1] Manual of Discipline, V, 1, 2.

[2] Thanksgiving Scroll, XIV, 14-22, pass. Tr. Theodore Gaster, The Dead Sea Scrolls, N.Y., 1956, p. 188-190.

[3] Philo, De Quod Probus Liber Sit, XII, 76.

[4] Cf. S. Lieberman, 'Light on the Cave Scrolls from Rabbinic Sources', Proceedings of the American Academy for Jewish Research, XX, 395-404.

[5] Josephus, Antiquities, XVIII, 1, 3.

[6] Hillel, cf. Avot, 2:5.

[7] Josephus, Jewish War, II, viii, 7.

[8] Mishnah and Tosefta Demai, Chs. 2 and 3. Cf. S. Lieberman, Tosefta Kipshuta, ad. loc. Cf. also Talmud Bavli, Bekorot 30b-31a.

[9] Cf. Mishnah Demai 2:2, 3; Tosefta Demai 2:2, 3, 10, 11; and Lieberman, op. cit. ad. loc. Cf. also S. Lieberman, 'Discipline in the so-called Dead Sea Manual of Discipline,' Journal of Biblical Literature, LXXI, 4 (1952), 199-206.

[10] Manual of Discipline V, 20-21.

[11] Zadokite Fragments 13:11, ed. Ch. Rabin, The Zadokite Fragments, Oxford 1954, 66.

[12] Mishnah Eduyot, 5:6-7.

[13] Avot 1:14.

II

FELLOWSHIP THROUGH LAW
The Haber

THE HABURAH (FELLOWSHIP) was as I have said a religious society founded in the villages and towns of Jewish Palestine during the Second Commonwealth in order to foster observance of the laws of tithing and ritual purity.[1] The sources on the fellowship are preserved in rabbinic literature, and the HABURAH has therefore been associated with the Pharisees; one must, nonetheless, retain the distinction between the HABURAH and the whole Pharisaic sect, since there is no evidence that all Pharisees were members of a fellowship.

Membership represented a status recognized by other members and not a formal affiliation with an organized society. The *haber* (member) of such a fellowship undertook to carry out even in the company of non-observant men those ritual laws which were generally neglected. Thus he taught their observance by example and precept. At the same time, the members distinguished themselves from the common society by their strict adherence to ritual laws which separated them in crucial relationships of daily life. Thus members cast up a barrier between themselves and the outsider, *Am-Ha-aretz*, who was by definition a source of ritual defilement.[2] The laws concerning food demanded more than what many men accepted as their proper religious obligation. The mass of farmers was careful to give heave-offering (*terumah gedolah*), but they did not always hand over the other agricultural dues to the priest and Levite.[3] Hence meticulously observant men had to take care to separate all necessary tithes and offerings.[4] Likewise the associates held that even secular food (*hulin*) had to be eaten in a state of ritual purity, and the masses of men did not do so.[5] Nonetheless, the Pharisaic traditions ascribed to the ancients the practice of eating even common food in a state of priestly purity,[6] and the commandments to tithe were biblically enjoined. This was, therefore, a natural concern for pious men.[7]

The member was a Jew who undertook to give all tithes and other sacred offerings from his foods and who undertook to preserve both for himself and others the ritual purity of his foods. Anyone might make such a commitment, man, woman, or child.[8] The fellowship cut across family ties. Wives might become members without their husbands, and children without their parents, though if a child was born into a family known to adhere to the rule, he was assumed to be observant until he indicated otherwise.[9] There were no caste distinctions, for some members of the priestly and Levitical castes were associates and others were not.[10] Furthermore not all Pharisees were adherents of the order; many kinds of men claimed to be Pharisees, and at both early and later periods, some sages were considered outsiders in relation to the fellowship.[11] A slave might become an associate and his master remain an outsider, and vice versa.[12] The specific rules of membership were exhaustive; whoever adhered to them became a member; beyond them, there were no distinctions between members and outsiders, and all outsiders were considered reliable on questions of ritual fitness of foods, even though they were not reliable to give evidence as to their ritual purity.[13]

Becoming a member of the order caused a revolution, therefore, in the life of the new member. Personal relationships had to be reconstructed, and new patterns of behaviour determined according to the specific regulations of the fellowship. The first obligation, for the outsider who entered into the status of 'reliability,' was to give all required tithes and heave-offerings. The second, for the 'initiate,' was to guard the ritual purity of these holy offerings, and in addition, to eat even secular produce in a state of ritual purity. In the third and final stage, the novice had to keep even those common foods he did not consume from ritual contamination, both at home and in commerce. A person entered the order by means of a formal undertaking, given unconditionally.[14] A newcomer might, however, proceed stage by stage to accept the obligations of a member, and he might at any point choose to go no further. He remained, in such a case, in his present status, and was not expelled from membership entirely. Such flexibility followed from the very purpose of the fellowship: to encourage Jews to fulfil neglected religious duties. At each stage, the newcomer reached a level of observance higher than before; if, therefore, he chose to remain only partially affiliated, this did not conflict with the purpose of the fellowship.

The primary sources on the process of entering the fellowship are as follows:

Mishnah Demai 2:2
    He that undertakes to be reliable must give tithe from what he eats and from what he sells and buys, and he may not be the guest of an outsider. R. Judah says, Even he that is the guest of an outsider may still be reckoned trustworthy. They replied, He would not be reliable in what concerns himself, how then could he be trustworthy in what concerns others?

Mishnah Demai 2:3
    He that undertakes to be a member may not sell to an outsider [foodstuff that is] wet or dry, nor buy from him [foodstuff that is] wet; and he may not be the guest of an outsider, nor may he receive him as a guest in his own garment.

Tosefta Demai 2:2

> He that imposes upon himself four things is accepted to be a member: not to give heave-offering or tithes to an outsider; not to prepare his pure food in the house of an outsider; and to eat even ordinary food in purity ...

Tosefta Demai 2:10-12.

> And he is accepted first with regard to 'wings' and is afterwards accepted for purities. If he only imposes upon himself the obligations concerning the 'wings' (cleanness of hands) he is accepted; if he imposes upon himself the obligations concerning pure food, but not concerning 'wings,' he is not considered reliable even for pure food.
>
> Until when is a man accepted? The school of Shamai say, For liquids, thirty days; for clothing, twelve months. The school of Hillel say, for either, thirty days.

The problem of defining the stages of affiliation is thus not simple. The Mishnah and Tosefta Demai give two different definitions, and the additional comments in the Tosefta require explanation. From Tosefta Demai 2:11 and 2:12, it is clear that there were several stages of entry into the fellowship.[15] An outsider had to conduct himself according to the rule of the fellowship, and afterwards was received for 'wings' and purities. He was nonetheless kept in the status of a novice with regard to liquids until after thirty days, and became a full member after twelve months (according to the school of Shamai). Professor Lieberman cites R. Jonah, who explains the difference between the definition of the Mishnah and that of the Tosefta by suggesting that the Tosefta deals with conditions to be fulfilled before one can be admitted, while the Mishnah deals with obligations incumbent on the established member.[16] It seems, rather, that the definitions of both texts deal with stages of affiliation before full membership. I suggest, following R. Jonah, that the Tosefta deals with the earliest stage, which would be an initiatory period; and the Mishnah deals with a later stage, which would be a novitiate. The description of the two stages of membership in Tosefta Demai 2:11 and 2:12 could, consequently, represent a broad definition of all the major concerns of the neophyte, and the Tosefta Demai 2:2 and Mishnah Demai 2:3 represent specific details incumbent on the newcomer. The sources relate, apparently, as follows:

Tosefta Demai 2:10	Tosefta Demai 2.2.
Purities	Not to give *terumah* and tithes to an outsider.
Purities	And not to prepare purities for and near an outsider.
Wings	And that he eat his common food in ritual purity and take upon himself to be trustworthy, tithing what he etc.
Tosefta Demai 2.11	Mishnah Demai 2.3.
Liquids	He does not sell an outsider wet or dry foods. And he does not acquire from him wet foods.
Garments	He does not accept the hospitality of an outsider. And does not receive him in his home in his (the outsider's) garment.

If this paradigm is a correct arrangement of the sources,[17] the stages of affiliating to the fellowship became clear. At the first stage of affiliation, the newcomer undertook to be reliable to give tithe from what he ate as well as from what he sold and purchased (from others for resale).[18] At the second level a reliable person entered the stage of initiation, in which he began to keep the laws of eating food in ritual purity.[19] Thus he began his affiliation by showing particular concern for ritual offerings, and for the purity of the food the initiate ate and prepared for himself. At the third stage, the novitiate, the newcomer undertook to guard the ritual purity of food under any circumstances; thus he could not sell any foodstuff (wet or dry), for in either case the outsider would contaminate the food by his touch, nor could he purchase from him food that is wet, and thus contaminated (moist produce was susceptible to uncleanness and dry produce was not), nor could he receive the outsider as a guest, on account of his contaminated garment. Following the period of reliability, the initiatory period was divided into two parts. First, the man became an initiate for 'wings,' that is, for the cleanness of his hands when he ate. Afterwards he obligated himself regarding 'purities,' that is, to preserve the sanctity of consecrated produce, withholding it from a priest or Levite who was an outsider, and who would probably consume the offerings in a state of impurity. In the novitiate, likewise, two periods punctuated entry into the fellowship. At first, the novice had to preserve his garments and liquid foods from ritual impurity, not allowing impurity to come upon any food in his possession or under his authority, by refraining from commerce in produce with outsiders, and by not purchasing from an outsider food that had been made ritually susceptible to uncleanness. At the same time, he had to take care to keep his garments from defilement, so that they might not contaminate his food; and he had to take care that the garments of outsiders did not touch his foodstuffs or defile them in any way. This novitiate lasted for thirty days in regard to both liquids and garments, according to the school of Hillel, or for thirty days in regard to liquids and twelve months in regard to garments, according to the school of Shamai. At the end of the three periods, of reliability, initiation, and the novitiate, the associate was considered dependable in all matters of tithes, of the ritual purity of his own food, of food he sold, and of his garments. Thus the following stages became apparent:

1. Reliability – (1) concern for tithing.
2. Initiation – (1) concern for tithing, and (2) for ritual purity of the initiate's own food, (2A) first for the cleanness of hands, and (2B) later for the cleanness of ritually-sacred foods.
3. Novitiate – (1) concern for tithing, (2) for ritual purity of the novice's own food, and (3) for food in his domain; and (4) (possibly) later, for the purity of his garment.

Some people conducted themselves privately according to the rule of the fellowship, particularly giving tithes meticulously. In such a case, a man was received immediately into the initiatory stage and instructed how to become a fully accredited member. If not, he was instructed, and only afterwards received into the initiatory stage.[20]

A later dispute may be illumined by this sequence of affiliation. During the latter half of the second century C.E., Rabbi Meir and Rabbi Judah disputed on whether a person in the status of reliability for tithes might accept the hospitality of an outsider and remain reliable. Rabbi Meir did not consider such hospitality permissible, apparently on account of the candidate's eating untithed food. Rabbi Judah answered, according to the same assumption, 'In all the days of householding, people never hesitated to eat in one another's homes, and even so, the produce in their own homes was properly tithed.' If, however, it was entirely possible for an individual to set aside tithes from the food which an outsider served him, and this is stated explicitly, then it is difficult to comprehend Rabbi Meir's tradition, prohibiting someone in the fellowship from accepting an outsider's hospitality. Apparently Rabbi Meir and Rabbi Judah held ancient traditions on the sequence of affiliation. Rabbi Meir's source forbade such hospitality, and Rabbi Judah's tradition was that such a prohibition against an outsider's hospitality did not apply at this stage (but rather at the later, novitiate level). Hence Rabbi Judah was correct, according to the sources, in disputing Rabbi Meir's contention that the hospitality of an outsider was forbidden to a reliable person; such hospitality was indeed prohibited to the novice, but on account of ritual contamination, not on account of tithes.[21] Indeed, it is explicitly stated that this prohibition did apply to the full member.[22]

After the destruction of the Temple, the fellowship apparently changed considerably; by the end of the second century C.E. the rule of the order ceased to be defined in its original terms at all. One discovers an elaboration of the conditions for becoming a fellow, 'R. Judah says, "He may not rear small cattle [a conservation measure], nor be profuse in vows of levity, nor contract corpse uncleanness, nor minister in the banquet hall." They said to him, "These things never came within the rule." ' This was correct, for the original articles of the fellowship did not cover such matters.[23]

A man who undertook to enter the fellowship had to do so before three members, although his dependents might declare their adherence before him. If he left the fellowship, he had to reassume these obligations upon return, if he might return at all. According to one opinion, if he violated his oath secretly, he was never eligible to reaffiliate, for he was a hypocrite. According to another, if he violated his oath secretly, then only by his own admission had he become suspect, and since a man's testimony against himself is discounted, he may indeed return in repentance; but if he violated his oath publicly, and others gave evidence against him, he might not re-enter the fellowship under any circumstances, as it is written (Jeremiah 3:14), 'Return, O faithless children . . .'[24] Furthermore a tax farmer was expelled from the moment he took his seals of office, although when he ceased to collect taxes, he could rejoin the association through a new, formal undertaking.[25]

The new member of the fellowship could no longer associate with any man freely and carelessly. In many ways he had to rearrange his habits of living into a new and complex pattern. The legal literature of the rabbinic period preserved many details of the relationship between members and outsiders. Obedience to the rule of the order meant that concern for the sanctity of foods entered into hitherto simple social relationships and the implications of this rule were translated, in minute detail, into everyday affairs. One principle governed every relationship: absolutely no compromise between the rule of the fellowship and the demands of the workaday world. The only exception, 'for the sake of peace,' was actually a mere leniency, and not a compromise at all.[26] At each of the three stages, the rule multiplied the problems bound up in living with men who were indifferent to obligations the member considered sacred. The fellowship chose to articulate the rule of the order, and to elaborate it to guide the member through the infinite, specific situations of daily life. These laws represented precise statements of the measure of the law, no more, no less. Such elaboration of law has been viewed with little sympathy by modern scholars, 'Nothing was left to the free personality, everything was placed under the bondage of the letter ... A healthy moral life could not flourish under such a burden. Action was nowhere the result of inward motive, all was, on the contrary, weighed and measured. Life was a continual torment to the earnest man, who felt at every moment that he was in danger of transgressing the law.'[27] This body of law was, however, fundamentally descriptive and enormously helpful. It was useful for people who adopted the rule of the fellowship, a rule they held as ancient and as sacred as the Ten Commandments, to know what to do and what not to do in the commonplace and homely situations of daily life. Having agreed, for example, to preserve the ritual purity of foodstuffs, the associate needed to know to what extent he was obligated to keep food only partially within his domain out of the hands of an outsider, in a common inheritance or in a joint agricultural or commercial enterprise. The formidable growth of law was a necessary consequence of the urban, unsegregated character of the fellowship. In the city and in the company of unobservant men, the potential range of problems to be solved by the fellowship rule was infinite. With precise and detailed information for guidance, the member might keep both his place in society and his sacred resolve.[28]

The fundamentally uncompromising[29] articulation of law became manifest in social, commercial, agricultural, and personal relationships.[30]

The member had, for example, to keep his cooking utensils out of possible contact with an outsider, who would render them unclean for several reasons.[31] Hence if he lived in the same courtyard with an outsider, he could not leave his vessels in the yard. He could not leave his pots or dishes in the domain or control of an outsider at any time.[32] On the other hand, an outsider was not suspect of touching the property of a member if he entered his domain without permission; he was presumptively careful not to contaminate the dwelling of a member.[33] If the member married the daughter of an outsider or purchased his slave, he had to adjure the newcomer to the rule of the order; if, on the other hand, his daughter or slave entered the domain of an outsider, the member was assumed to remain observant until proven otherwise. In any case the undertaking had to be renewed.[34] A man might enter the fellowship without his wife; if he was reliable (for tithes) and his wife was not, then associates might purchase food from him, but might not accept his hospitality, for he was as one who lives 'in the same basket with a snake.' If his wife was reliable and he was not, then associates might accept his hospitality but not purchase food from him.[35]

Family relationships were no less complex. In matters of inheritance, the associate might make no exchange of food with an outsider who shared his inheritance; but he might say, 'Take the wheat there, and I shall take this wheat here,' leaving to the outsider food that was either ritually unclean or susceptible to impurity, and keeping the ritually clean food for himself. He might not be the direct cause of an outsider's receiving food.[36] The son of a member might visit the non-observant members of his parents' families, so long as the outsiders did not give him unclean food. If they did, he would defile his own home, and hence might not visit his relatives any longer. Hospitality was difficult; if, for instance, a man 'left an outsider within the house awake, and found him awake, or asleep and found him asleep, or awake and found him asleep, the house remained clean [the possibility that the outsider moved about and contaminated the house is discounted], but if he left him asleep and found him awake, the house is unclean, according to Rabbi Meir, or that part of the house is unclean which he could touch by stretching out his hand, according to the sages.[37] Apparently the outsider was considered normally careful not to defile the house of the associate, as was seen above, for here again it would not be possible to allow him to remain alone in a member's home at all. A fellow of the order could not in any case accept the hospitality of an outsider, or receive him into his own home unless he put on ritually clean garments.[38] While a member could not prepare for an outsider any kind of food, and vice versa, an outsider might still watch the pot of a member; he might not add spices. Wives of members and of outsiders might prepare food together under conditions of extreme caution.[39] In any case, the word of an outsider on the ritual purity of food or on its condition with regard to tithes and heave-offerings was accepted when he spoke en passant or in his innocence.[40] An outsider might not act as the agent of a fellow, or vice versa, in any matter to do with foodstuffs, although the outsider might act as agent of the member to purchase dry stuffs when the act was clearly specified in advance ('Buy me cabbages from the corner store and from no one else').[41] If a member left his produce in the care of an outsider, the food remained in its presumptive state of tithes and heave-offerings, but it was rendered unclean if it was moist. If an outsider entered an associate's house, 'such time as the member can see them that go in and out, only foodstuffs and liquids and open earthenware vessels become unclean, but if the householder could not see them that go in and out, even though the outsider could not move himself or was tied up, all becomes unclean.'[42]

Commercial relations were similarly transformed. It was difficult for a member of the fellowship to sell foodstuffs, for his only customers could be other members (but there is no evidence that members refrained from such commerce entirely). A farmer, for example, might sell olives only to another associate, according to the opinion of the Shamaites, and although the school of Hillel permits him to sell to a reliable person, still the scrupulous members of the latter school followed the opinion of the school of Shamai. There were other limitations on what foods the member might sell to outsiders under any circumstances; on the other hand, members might bring their grain to an unaffiliated miller, since grain was dry-milled. They might also employ outsiders in their foodshops, since their rules were presumably obeyed; and if an associate was in partnership with an outsider, other members might still purchase food at the shop and assume that the member had removed the proper tithes. If the associate took a field as share-cropper, he had to give tithes for his landlord, deducting them from the latter's share; under certain circumstances, the associate-landlord had to tithe the crops of his non-observant tenants from his own share. Finally, a journeyman-member might study a craft with an unaffiliated master and vice versa; in the latter case, the journeyman was considered observant of all rules of the fellowship during his working hours, but if he wanted to enter the order, he had to give a formal undertaking.[43]

Just as a member of the fellowship could not give priestly or Levitical dues to an outsider, so he could not present his first-fruits to an outsider, or repay to an unaffiliated priest any fines or recompense due to the priesthood for misuse of priestly produce. The associate had to pay fines to a priest of the fellowship, and the latter compensated the unaffiliated priest for the produce he had lost. If the consecrated produce of priests was mixed together, then the associate had to purchase the share of the outsider (unlike the situation of joint inheritance). The garments of an outsider could not, of course, come into contact with consecrated food; if they did, the priest had to burn the produce.[44]

While these laws indicate the configuration of rules which guided the fellowship, they do not by any means exhaust the vast legal literature relevant directly or indirectly to the life of the members.[45] Membership in the fellowship was achieved through a pattern of actions which demonstrated the initiate's devotion to certain neglected Jewish traditions. Dedicated to keep the ordinances on tithing and the purity of foods, the associates defined the rule of their fellowship, educated newcomers in the manner to keep it, and determined a sequence of obligations by which an outsider might learn by degrees to enter into the full observance of the Jewish faith. With neither a formal organization nor a sovereign authority to enforce a man's undertaking, the members of the fellowship followed the teaching of Shamai, 'Say little and do much!'[46]

NOTES AND REFERENCES

[1] J. Baumgarten, 'Qumran Studies,' Journal of Biblical Literature, LXXVII, 3, 249-257, states, 'All in all it seems quite difficult to make out of the haburah anything more than a society for the strict observance of ritual cleanliness.' I have found no evidence to contradict Dr. Baumgarten's judgment. On the contrary, there is no indication that all Pharisees were members of a fellowship, although all members were Pharisees and accepted their views on Jewish law. There is, furthermore, no indication in the sources I have examined that the fellowship was an organized society at all, with officers or a formal governing body. A person became a member by stating his intention to keep the rules of the fellowship before three old members; he entered into the framework of obligations membership imposed. Membership thus entailed nothing more than a recognized status.

[2] Buechler's thesis (cf. A. Buechler, Der Galilaische Am Ha-Ares des Zweiten Jahrhunderts, Vienna, 1906) that the laws of ritual purity and strict tithing applied primarily to members of the priestly cast achieved

some popularity among historians of this period. This thesis has been demolished by G. Allon in his essay, cited in detail below, 'The Application of the Laws on Ritual Purity' (cf. G. Allon, Researches in the History of Israel, Tel Aviv, 1957, I, 148-177). Buechler thought that the extension of these laws to the common people took place in the second century C.E.; because of the rabbis' bitterness at the Hadrianic persecutions, they devised these laws to separate the Jewish people once for all from the gentile world. Allon discusses and refutes this thesis as well.

[3] The common people apparently recognized the biblical injunction to give heave-offering (cf. T. B. Sotah 48a), but were not careful to separate other offerings.

[4] Significantly, the laws concerning the Pharisaic fellowship were inserted in the tractate on 'doubtful produce' (*demai*), the doubt being whether produce has been fully and properly tithed. The observance of these laws involved separating first-tithe and heave-offering of the tithe, as well as second-tithe, to be eaten in Jerusalem, and poor-man's tithe (these last were given alternately, in the seven-year cycle, years one, two, four and five were for second-tithe, three and six for poor-man's tithe). On the enactment of the laws of 'doubtful produce,' cf. Sotah 48a (Mishnah Maaser Sheni, 5:15); C. Albeck, Seder Zeraim (Tel Aviv, 1957), 69-70; and especially, S. Lieberman, Hellenism in Jewish Palestine (New York, 1950), p. 143, note 28.

[5] All men ought to remain ritually pure, according to rabbinic sources. Cf. Allon, op. cit., pp. 169-176. Ritual purity was a widespread obsession. Cf. *inter alia*, the following: Philo, De Specialibus Legibus, III, 205; Josephus, Contra Apion, 2:26; Antiquities III, xi, 3; cf. especially W. Brandt, Juedische Reinheitslehre und Ihre Beschreibung in den Evangelien (Giessen, 1910), pp. 1-55; and also J. Harrison, Prolegomena to the Study of Greek Religion (Cambridge, 1903), pp. 24-29; M. Nilsson, History of Greek Religion (2nd ed., Oxford), pp. 84-85, 218-220. Buechler states (in 'Levitical Impurity of the Gentile in Palestine before the year 70,' Jewish Quarterly Review, n.s. XVII, 80-81), 'They assumed that Levitical impurity of the gentile affected only the priest on duty [in the Temple] and the ordinary Jew only when he was ritually pure for a visit to the Temple and for participation in a sacrificial meal. The private associations between Jew and gentile were in no way restricted, and commercial and other relations were not affected by the Levitical purity ascribed to the gentile.' On p. 48 of the same article, Buechler asks, 'Is there any, even the slightest indication in rabbinic literature that the touch of a gentile caused a defilement, and that such a defilement was taken into account by the strictest Jew not an Essene in Temple times?' One such indication at least will be found in Mishnah Avodah Zarah 4:9. The reason for the prohibition is obviously that the Jew will assist the gentile in the process by which grapes become susceptible to contamination and the gentile will forthwith – by touch – contaminate them! (Buechler would argue that this applies only to the priest, but no evidence supports this view.) Cf. also Tosefta Makshirin

3:7. Allon discusses this *mishnah* (op cit., p. 161, note 59), and states that the sages regarded ritual purity as the obligation of every Jew; since many did not keep the laws of purity, the sages 'found it necessary . . . to seek out the company [of observant men] and to set themselves apart by means of a formal act of undertaking, to fulfil meticulously these laws.' Cf. also TB Hullin 2:6; and the dispute of the schools of Hillel and Shamai, TB Berakot 8:2, 3, in which all parties agree that it is forbidden to render foods unclean during a meal, disagreeing on the best means to prevent impurity.

[6] Abraham ate his secular food in ritual purity, TB Baba Metsiah 87a; B'reshit Rabbah, ch. 44. For Saul, cf. Midrash Tehilim, ps. 7, ed. Buber, p. 32a; Pesikta de R. Kavana, ed. Buber, 78; Pesikta Rabbati, ch. 15 ed. Friedman, p. 68a. For a complete discussion of this question, cf. Buechler, op. cit., pp. 119-124, and Allon, op. cit., pp. 158-169, esp. p. 159, note 52.

[7] Cf. for example the view of Philo, De Specialibus Legibus, III, 205.

[8] Cf. Tosefta Demai 2:2-3:10, pass., S. Lieberman, Tosefta Kipshutah (N.Y., 1955), *ad loc.* Specific citations follow.

[9] The fellows cut across family lines, cf. Tos. Dem. 2:15, 16, 17, 3:5, 9.

[10] The distinction between member priests and Levites and others is implicit in Mishnah Demai 2:2, 3 and Tos. Demai 2:2, 3. There is no apparent economic distinction either; at least, according to Tos. Demai 2:19, a journeyman apprentice is a member and his craftsman-teacher is not (and vice versa); cf. also Tos. Demai 3:5, 3:9, 2:15.

[11] Seven kinds of Pharisee are listed in Sotah 22a (TP Sotah 5:7; cf. TP Berakot 9:7). Cf. also Tos. Demai 2:13, the opinion of Abba Shaul, and the parallel passage in Bekorot 30a; and Professor Lieberman's comment, op. cit., ad loc. Cf. also TP Demai 2:3 and Professor Lieberman's comment and emendation to the passage, Tarbiz, XX, 110-111: A sage in Babylon tells some women to be cautious in approaching him, for he is in the status of an outsider in relationship to ritual purities; cf. also L. Finkelstein, Introduction to the Treatises Abot and Abot of Rabbi Nathan, New York, 1950, p. 243.

[12] Tos. Demai 3:6, 3:9; TP Demai 2:2 *inter alia*.

[13] TP Demai 2:3. This is a point often misunderstood in secondary works on this period.

[14] Tos. Demai 2:3, Bekorot 30a. Cf. Lieberman, op. cit., p. 211, note 9. Cf. also Tos. Dem. 2:13, TP Dem. 2:3; Bekorot 30b on the formal undertaking. The undertaking is a kind of vow or oath, cf. Lieberman, op. cit. p. 217. For the possibility of accepting only the first obligation of membership, cf. Tos. Dem. 2:3, 5, II.

[15] Lieberman, op. cit., p. 216, para. 37.

[16] Cf. also Rabin, op. cit., p. 12, note 7.

[17] According to this interpretation of the several sources, wings, purities, liquids, and garments in Tos. Demai 2:II, 12, have specific meanings as detailed below. The following evidence supports this explanation:

Wings means 'washing of hands' according to Professor Lieberman and earlier commentators. Cf. Lieberman, op. cit., pp. 215-216; Bekorot 30a and Rashi *ad loc.*; the Aruk HaShalem, listed under Professor Lieberman, explains this unusual usage by reference to Kelim 17:14, Tos. Kel. B.M. 7:5; TP Nazir 4:10 (TB Nazir 46b).

Purities comprehends both concern for the ritual purity of food that the initiate eats (i.e., that he will not prepare pure foodstuffs near an outsider), but also concern for preserving the purity of consecrated food. For a similar ambiguity, cf. Oholot 18:2, Bekorot 3:II, 3:2, 3:13. This latter connotation is preserved in TP Demai 2:2 by Rav Mana, who equates 'purities' with 'tithes.' Furthermore, Kossovsky (Concordance to the Tosefta, Jerusalem, 1939) states that 'purities' in the Tosefta connotes anything which is done or preserved in ritual purity; for the detailed meaning of 'purities' in the TP passage cited, cf. Lieberman, op. cit., p. 215.

Liquids in Tractate Makshirin connotes 'that which renders dry produce susceptible to become impure', precisely the meaning assigned here. Cf. *inter alia* Makshirin I:I, 6:4, and Albeck, Seder Taharot (Tel Aviv, 1959), p. 411. The word MŠKH as used in Leviticus 11:34 was interpreted by the rabbis to mean a liquid (one of seven) capable of rendering dry produce susceptible to impurity; hence liquids in Tos. Demai 2:11 connotes concern not to bring a liquid into contact with dry produce. Parallel usages are in Pesahim 17b, Terumot II:2, etc. Liquids likewise implies, and as its primary meaning, concern to protect the purity of liquids.

Garments means, according to Rashi (Bekorot 30b-31a; cf. also Lieberman, op. cit., *ad loc.*) that the novice must learn to keep his garment in the state of purity appropriate to an associate. Cf. Mishnah Hagigah, ch. 2 at the end; for an instance of such concern, cf. Tos. Taharot 5:16. If the novice accepts the hospitality of an outsider, he will render his garment unclean by virtue of the uncleanness of the chairs; when the outsider is dressed in his own garments, he is a source of impurity, for his garments can render an object unclean when they are carried (cf. Hagigah 2:7). The general term garments in Tos. Demai 2:II apparently connotes these two specific details. Cf. also Mishnah Taharot, 4:5.

For another explanation of the difference between the two definitions, cf. L. Finkelstein, *The Pharisees* (Philadelphia, 1938), II, p. 662.

[18] Tos. Demai 2:3, Mishnah Demai 2:2. In the matter of tithes, the reliable person must not only keep the laws himself, but he must keep others from transgressing as well. In the second stage, the initiate must keep only his own food in a state of ritual purity. The novice, however, must be careful for others as well.

[19] Tos. Demai 2:2, following Professor Lieberman's emendation. Cf. Lieberman, op. cit., p. 210, notes 4 and 5.

[20] On private conformity to the rule, cf. Lieberman, op. cit., p. 214. I only propose this interpretation as most sensible, for if the newcomer was immediately received into the final stage of membership in the

order, how was he to carry out the complicated observance of ritual purity 'as he goes along?' He could, on the other hand, certainly give the necessary tithes and heave-offerings without further instruction. Hence I propose that the initial reception was into the stage of reliability, and he was instructed, 'as he goes along,' in the responsibilities of the initiate.

[21] I have found no support for this hypothesis.

[22] Mishnah Demai 2:3.

[23] For evidence of this change in the nature of the fellowship, cf. Sotah 9:15; Tos. Shabbat I:7; Bekorot 30b; Lieberman, op. cit., p. 216, para. 40, states, 'According to the tradition of the Babylonian Talmud, Abba Shaul hands on an ancient law, but afterwards, when the Temple was destroyed, the standards of ritual purity (observed by the priests) were raised, so as not to place credence in any man, even a sage.' Professor Lieberman cites Maimonides, The Book of Cleanness, Laws of Commonwealth (Tel Aviv, 1953), III, 119; and the extensive variations in the definition of the fellow Bekorot 47b.

Rabbi Judah's definition is emended by J. N. Epstein, Introduction to Tannaitic Literature (Jerusalem – Tel Aviv, 1957) to read as presented here; cf. Rabin, op. cit., p. 12, note 9. Rabin's treatment of the rule of the novitiate varies considerably from the view presented here. Rabin, op. cit., 18-20.

[24] Cf. Bekorot 31a; Tos. Demai 2:9, and Lieberman, op. cit., *ad loc.* TP Demai 2:3; TB Avodah Zarah 7a, and the comment of the Tosafot there. I follow Professor Lieberman's comment, op. cit., p. 214, paras. 28-29.

[25] Tos. Demai 3:9; TB Bekorot 31a; TP Demai 2:3; Lieberman, op. cit., p. 224, paras. 15-17.

[26] Mishnah Gittin 5:9 (parallel in Shevi-it 5:9; TB Gittin (61a).

[27] E. Schuerer, History of the Jewish People in the Time of Jesus Christ (Edinburgh, 1894), II, pp. 102, 106-107, 124. For other viewpoints on the *halachah* in general, cf. R. Herford, The Pharisees (London, 1924); G. F. Moore, Judaism (Cambridge, 1954), Finkelstein, op. cit.; cf. also Tractate Avot, pass., and Psalm 19:7-14.

[28] Finkelstein, op. cit., I 74-75, and the same author's article in the Harvard Theological Review, XXII, 209-210.

[29] This is not to imply that the Pharisaic viewpoint was extreme. On the contrary, the tendency was, on the whole, moderate, given the range of possibilities that presented themselves to the sages. Cf. for many examples, Tractate Kelim, pass., and the Code of Maimonides, Book of Cleanness (Book Ten), tr. Danby (Yale Judaica Series, Vol. VIII; N. H., 1954), particularly the preface of Professor Julian Obermann (pp. v-xiv), and the introduction by Canon Danby (pp. xxxiii-xlv); also the commentary Eliyahu Rabbah to the Sixth Division of the Mishnah by the Gaon Rabbi Elijah of Vilna, in Danby, The Mishnah (Oxford, 1933), pp. 800-804; and cf. also the comment of Allon, op. cit., p. 176, who suggests that the following pattern is discernible in the disputes on ritual purity: the Sadducees demanded the strictest possible inter-

pretation of the laws of ritual purity, but limited the application of these laws to the priests in the Temple itself; the Essenes likewise interpreted the laws very strictly, and applied them to every situation in daily life, but separated themselves into communes of observant men and women; among the Pharisees, the tendency to apply the laws of purity to daily life conflicted with the impulse to limit severely the laws of purity. Allon continues, 'There were two basic principles guiding the Pharisees; one, to make the law congruent to the needs of the living, and the other, to extend the principle of sanctity to every man (not only the priests) and to every place (not only the Temple). The second principle obligated the sages to teach Israel to observe ritual purity, and to demand complete separation [from uncleanness]. However, life demanded the limitation of these laws, for it is not possible, or at least very inconvenient, to keep them. Therefore ... the traditions, such as washing hands before a meal, which were not difficult to keep, or which were particularly crucial, such as the prohibitions concerning women in the menstrual period, were carried out.' For a discussion of the implications of the laws of purity in economic life, cf. L. Ginzberg, Jewish Law and Lore (Philadelphia, 1955), pp. 79-84, 109, 113, 120-122; S. Zeitlin, History of the Second Jewish Commonwealth, Prolegomena (Philadelphia, 1933). Professor Zeitlin discusses the modification of the laws of purity for the sake of convenience, and concludes, 'The Pharisees from time to time modified the *halakot* in order to make the law accord with the requirements and demands of life.'

The entire question of the sociological application of the laws of ritual purity has by no means been exhausted. It would be worthwhile, for one thing, to know in detail and through a study of texts (*contra* Schuerer) what these laws actually meant in the daily life of the Palestinian Jew during the several major epochs of the *halachah* in the Second Commonwealth and afterwards; and for another, what were the principles that governed the articulation and elaboration of the laws of purity.

[30] This is merely a brief summary of certain social relationships affected by the fellowship and its rule. A complete survey would entail not only a study of the specific laws which deal with the relationship of member and outsider, but also a consideration of each of the laws of ritual purity and impurity.

[31] Midrash-uncleanness, Maddaf-uncleanness, etc. Cf. Toh. 8:2, and Maimonides, Book of Uncleanness, *ad loc.*

[32] Taharot 8:1, 2, 3.

[33] Ibid., 8:5.

[34] Tos. Demai 2:16, 17 parallel TB Avodah Zarah 39a; Tos. Avodah Zarah 3:9; Bekorot 30b. Cf. Lieberman, op. cit., *ad loc.*

[35] Tos. Demai 3:9; cf. TP Demai 2:2. For the expression 'dwell with a serpent,' cf. TB Ketuvot 71a. For problems of an associate who worked as a house servant of an outsider, cf. Tos. Demai 3-6; TP Demai 2:2. The servant had to see to tithing the food, and if it was known that the waiter was a member, then the affiliated guests might

assume that the food had been tithed. But it is most important to note that a member might in fact work for an outsider, and even serve food to his table.

[36] Mishnah Demai 6:8, 9.

[37] Tos. Demai 2:15, 3:5 (parallel TB Yevamot 114a). If the child ate unclean food at the relative's, he could render his own home unclean. Cf. Taharot 2:2.

[38] Tos. Demai 2:2, 3.

[39] Tos. Maaserot 3:13; Tos. Demai 4:29, 3:1, 2:2, 4:31, 32. Tos. Demai 4:27 (compare 2:2). Mishnah Taharot 7:4.

[40] Tos. Demai 2:24; Maaserot 5:2; Mishnah Makshirin 6:3. Cf. also Tos. Demai 5:5; Mishnah Demai, 4:6.

[41] Tos. Demai 2:20, 2:21, 2:22, 3:2. Compare 4:26, 5:3, 8:1. Mishnah Demai 6:22; Tos. Demai 8:1.

[42] Tos. Demai 4:22, 28; Mishnah Taharot 7:5. Cf. also ibid., 7:1, 2; 8:1, 2.

[43] Mishnah Demai 6:6; Tos. Demai 2:3 (Mishnah Demai 2:2). Cf. Tos. Demai 3:15. Other sources include the following: Tos. Demai 2:18-19, 3:5, 8, 9; Mishnah Demai 3:4, 6:1, 8. Cf. also Mishnah Terumot 3:4, Maaserot 3:13, 7:12.

[44] Bikkurim 3:12; Tos. Demai 3:1, 2, 3, 5; Mishnah Demai 2:2, 3; Tos. Terumot 7:4; TP Terumot 6:1; Mishnah Taharot 4:5.

[45] For other references, cf. the following, *inter alia*, in the TB: Berakot 36b, 40b, 47b; Shabbat 13a, 32a; Erubin 37a, b; Pesahim 4a, b; Yoma 8b; Moed Katan 22b, 26b-27a; Hagigah 18b, 22a, 23a, 24b, 25a, 26a; Kiddushin 33b; 56a, b; Sotah 49a, b; Sanhedrin 8b, 40a, 72b, 90b; Avodah Zarah 7a, b, 39a, 41b, 42a, 64b, 70b; Makkot 6b (parallel Sanhedrin 8b), 9b; Shevuot 16a; Niddah 6b, 15b, 33b; Kelim 9:2 (parallel Eduyot 1:14); Oholot 5:5 (cf. Hagigah 3:4, Parah 5:1); Makshirin 6:3; Zabim 3:2, Taharot 7:4.

On the question of whether the fellowship had some kind of communal meal, cf. Pesahim 113b, and the discussion of Rabin, op. cit., p. 32; Rabin cites Mishnah Sanhedrin 8:2, and the statement of A. Geiger in 'Sadducaer und Pharisaer' (Jud. Zeitschrift, 1868, p. 25). Rabin says, 'Nothing in the context of Tosefta Demai suggests that the *haburah* held common meals, but we must remember that the word can also be employed in a general way for a group holding a common meal in connexion with some religious occasion ... With all due reserve I think that the new evidence of the scrolls gives grounds for reviving Geiger's theory that the common meals formed an essential part of *haburah* life and influenced various features of Pharisee practice ...' The relationship of the fellowship to the *haburah Shel mitzvah* is not yet clear; the fellowship discussed here may be simply one example of such societies or status-groups formed to carry out particular religious obligations.

[46] Avot I:15.

III

FELLOWSHIP THROUGH INTELLECT

The Talmid Hakham

A SECOND KIND of fellowship existed among the Pharisees, the fellowship of learning men. It may best be described through the particular social entity embodied in the circle of disciples that gathered around Rabban Yohanan ben Zakkai (c. 1-80 C.E.).[1] At Jerusalem Rabban Yohanan assembled a circle of disciples to whom he taught Torah, thus constituting a social group founded on the study and application of biblical literature. Master and disciples brought to Scripture questions which touched on moral, legal, ethical, and ritual matters. Through study of Scripture, they sought to find guidance on the conduct of daily affairs, believing that in commonplace actions, the crucial and consequential issues of life were decided. Indeed, the very act of study represented both content and form in Yohanan's religious doctrine. He spent most of his life in study, and through such study, he taught how to live:

> If thou hast wrought much in the study of Torah, do not claim merit for thyself, for to this end wast thou created.[2]

Study of Torah provided an alternate focus for religious life to either cultic ritual or charismatic action. The priests thought to do God's will through the Temple rites, the ecstatics and miracle-workers by prayer and meditation, and Yohanan and the other sages, by memorizing, interpreting (or, sometimes misinterpreting), and applying ancient texts. These texts were believed to contain the secret to the inner structure of reality; through them, one came to an understanding of the whole of existence, and therefore, to an apprehension of the divine will in creation. Torah made manifest the universal design and plan for existence:

> 'The Lord made me as the beginning of his way, the first of his works of old. I was set up from everlasting, from the beginning or even the earth was made ... when he marked out the foundations of the earth, then I was beside him, like a master workman; I was daily his delight, rejoicing before him always.' (Prov. 8:22-30 pass.) The Torah says, 'I was God's instrument. According to the custom of the world, when a mortal king builds a palace, he does not build it by his own skill, but with the skill of an architect. And that architect does not build it out of his own head, but employs plans and diagrams in order to know how to arrange the chambers and wicket doors. So too did the Holy One, blessed be He, He looked into the Torah and created the world.[3]

The idea of Torah rested on the notion that the world presented an order and regularity which man might uncover through the study of revelation, the source of insight into the cosmos. In studying Torah, therefore, a man studied the divine architect's plan for life itself, and achieved the possibility to penetrate into life's meaning. Study of Torah may have been an act of intellect, but when Yohanan taught that it was to this end that man was created, he manifested more than an intellectual dedication to the exposition of ancient revelation. He proposed, rather, what was a religious programme: if God was transcendent, his word was immanent, and the sage and disciple should serve him through study of that word.

This programme was not, of course, Yohanan's invention. The ideal of Torah was held, for example, by Ben Sira, three centuries earlier. For Ben Sira, however, the achievement of 'Wisdom' depended on the leisure and means to support study. It is instructive to note, therefore, how this ideal had become transformed in the intervening centuries from that of the upper-class intellectual to that of the generally poorer sage:

> The wisdom of the scribe depends on the opportunity of leisure, And he who has little business may become wise (Ben Sira 39:1-5).[4]

Ben Sira promised that the sage, a kind of *magus* in his view, would have a great career, appear before rulers, travel far and wide:

> He will serve among great men and appear before rulers
> He will travel through the lands of foreign nations
> For he tests the good and the evil among men
> (Ben Sira 39:4-5).[5]

While some of the sages, particularly Gamaliel I, Simeon ben Gamaliel, and Josephus (who claimed to adhere to the Pharisaic party) did pursue public careers, and Yohanan himself served among the great men of Jerusalem, for the most part the sages did not find public careers open to them, and did not travel abroad. They were mostly poor, and appeared before rulers only when the tax-farmer hailed them into court. Yohanan himself did, however, see the fulfilment of one of Ben Sira's promises:

> If he lives long, he will leave a name greater than a thousand, And if he goes to rest, It is enough for him (Ben Sira 39:11).[6]

If the sage merited long life, he could hope to leave a lasting monument, but if he died before his time, he could at least say, 'Enough, I have had my portion in the Torah.'[7]

Study of Torah yielded more than moral and religious benefit. It created a community, bringing student and teacher together; sitting, walking, travelling by the way, the sages speculated together on momentous matters. This fellowship of interested men represented another kind of polity in the urban, anomic situation. Like the Pharisaic fellowship (*haburah*), the Nazarene community in Jerusalem, and the monastery at Qumran,[8] it entailed a social commitment: among these men and in their society, the spiritual life will be lived. Such a social group was not unique, for the pagan world had long witnessed the formation of societies for the communal study of religious and intellectual problems.[9] Speculative problems, studied by Academic and Peripatetic masters and their disciples, had, however, long ago given way to the deepening concern for moral issues. Ancient metaphysical perplexities were left behind, for, with the end of the corporate life of ancient cities, ancestral laws and institutions lost their cloak of almost divine authority, and the moral supports of society became the focus of men's concern. Indeed, the individual was thrown upon his own resources, and the great problems of philosophy centred upon how to achieve autonomy of character.[10] Not only in the land of Israel, but throughout the world men had been uprooted from their ancient foundations.[11] The sensitive among them experienced profound alienation from their past, and from their contemporaries in the present. Submerged into the masses of men in the metropolitan cities, they lacked adequate expression for their individuality. Those who were able to find new expression for their own souls, such as the sages of Israel and of the nations, had to speak to a new social setting, and provide their disciples with a new corporate society to explore the implications of ancient wisdom for daily affairs. The academy was thus both a school for life and, at the same time, the setting for individual living and for the expression of the private person's individuality. Opportunities for such self-expression were no longer easily available in the common life of the city; the end of the corporate community of the ancient city, in which each man had his place and his hour, created undifferentiated masses, and from such masses came men seeking for themselves a means of individual and social expression.

In Rome, such uprooted men found for themselves a kind of spiritual or moral master who would impart the 'art of life.' Such a moral director was qualified by his profound knowledge of the pathology of the soul, and offered private counsel, much as the analyst does today, for the particular needs of his spiritual patient. He encouraged his charge to 'make full confession of the diseases of his soul,' trained him in moral self-examination, and tried to help him find the way to right living in a world gone wrong.[12] The goal was to produce the *sapiens*, who was the man who sees in the light of Eternal Reason the true proportions of things, whose affections have been trained to obey the higher law, whose will has hardened into an unswerving conformity to it in all the difficulties of conduct, and the true philosopher is no longer the cold, detached student of intellectual problems far removed from the struggles and miseries of human life. He has become the *generis humani paedagogus*, the schoolmaster to bring men to the Ideal Man. . . .[13]

There could be no more congruent description of the task assumed by Yohanan ben Zakkai and his colleagues, but, in characteristically Jewish fashion, he found 'eternal reason' in the Torah, looked for the 'higher law' in ancient revelation, and would bring men not to the ideal man, but closer to the Father in Heaven. If Seneca, who was Yohanan's contemporary, thought to root character in a faith in the rational law of conduct, Yohanan saw the foundation of all natural law in the Torah. Both would have agreed, however, that freedom is achieved through conformity to the higher part of being, the vision of which provides universal laws for particular actions. Both tried to make a place where men might once again matter.

Since Yohanan's conception of the good life was to learn a sacred text and its interpretation, the form of the good society which he created for his disciples was the academy; his sole credential as master was his learning; and his main function was to teach. His main pedagogical technique was the hoary method of catechism. He would ask questions and hear answers; he would be asked questions and provide answers. On occasion, he gave a wrong answer, which was interpreted as an effort to keep his students alert. He was asked:

> In what garments is the heifer prepared? He said, in golden garments. The students replied, but have you not taught us, master, in white garments? He answered, If I have forgotten what I saw with my own eyes and did with my own hands, how much the more what I taught! Why did he go to such an extent? In order to keep the students alert. And there are those who say, this was Hillel the Elder, but that he could not say, what my own hands did.[14]

On a second occasion, he tried to make his nephew's misfortune yield a spiritual truth, that philanthropy must be done for its own sake. It was reported as follows:

> Rabbi Judah son of Rabbi Shalom preached as follows: In the same way as a man's earnings are determined for him from New Year, so his losses are determined for him from New Year. If not, then he will 'bring the poor that are outcast to his house.' A case in point is that of the nephews of Rabban Yohanan ben Zakkai. He saw in a dream that they were to lose seven hundred dinars in that year. He accordingly forced them to give money for charity, until only seventeen dinars were left of the seven hundred. On the eve of the day of Atonement, the Government sent and seized them. Rabban Yohanan ben Zakkai said to them, Do not fear (that you will lose any more). You had seventeen dinars, and these they have taken. They said to him, How did you know that this was going to happen? He replied, I saw it in a dream. And why did you not tell us, they asked. Because, he said, I wanted you to perform the religious precept without ulterior motive.[15]

FELLOWSHIP THROUGH INTELLECT

Yohanan ben Zakkai had five disciples in his circle in Jerusalem. For each he had a name:

> Eliezer ben Hyrcanus he called 'plastered cistern' which loses not a drop, pitch-coated flask, which keeps its wine. Joshua ben Hananiah he called three-fold cord not quickly broken. Yosi the Priest he called 'the generation's saint.' Simeon ben Natanel he called 'oasis in the desert which holds on to its water.' And Eleazar ben Arakh he called 'overflowing stream and ever-flowing stream whose waters ever flow and overflow' – confirming the statement, 'Let thy springs be dispersed abroad, and courses of water in the streets.' (Prov. 5.16.)

For one, he had very special praise:

> He used to say, 'If all the sages of Israel were in one scale of the balance, and Rabbi Eliezer ben Hyrcanus were in the other scale, he would outweigh them all. Abba Shaul says in his name, If all the sages of Israel were in one scale of the balance, and even if Rabbi Eliezer ben Hyrcanus were with them, and Rabbi Eleazar ben Arakh were in the other scale, he would outweigh them all.[16]

Much like the philosophical director in Seneca's Rome, Yohanan would discourse with his students on basic questions facing moral man. Yohanan phrased his questions in universal terms. He sought an ethic applicable to all men and in all places. Yohanan asked 'what is the good way of life,' and 'what is the evil way of life,' always phrasing his moral inquiries in terms applicable to all men. In each case, he demanded observation of life as it was lived, telling his disciples to go out and see the world for themselves. Thus it was reported that he told them:

> Go out and see which is the good way to which a man should cleave, so that through it he may enter the world to come.

The students returned with their conclusions:

> Rabbi Eliezer came in and said, a good eye (that is liberality).
> Rabbi Joshua came in and said, A good companion.
> Rabbi Yosi came in and said, A good neighbour, a good impulse and a good wife.
> Rabbi Simeon came in and said, Foresight.
> Rabbi Eleazar came in and said, Good-heartedness toward heaven, and goodheartedness toward the commandments, and goodheartedness toward mankind.
> Rabban Yohanan said to them, I prefer the words of Rabbi Eleazar ben Arakh to your words, for in his words, your words are included.

Again, he instructed the students:

> Go out and see which is the evil way which a man should shun, so that he may enter the world to come.

The students again returned:

> Rabbi Eliezer came in and said, An evil eye (that is, avarice).
> Rabbi Joshua came in and said, An evil companion.
> Rabbi Yosi came in and said, An evil neighbour, and evil impulse, and an evil wife.
> Rabbi Simeon came in and said, Borrowing and not repaying, for he that borrows is as one who borrows from God, as it is said The wicked borroweth and payeth not, but the righteous dealeth graciously and giveth (Ps. 37.21).
> Rabbi Eleazar came in and said, Meanheartedness toward heaven and meanheartedness toward the commandments, and meanheartedness toward mankind.

To this Yohanan replied:

> I prefer the words of Rabbi Eleazar to your words, for in his words, your words are included.[17]

Eleazar's recommendation of 'wholeheartedness,' or a good heart, recalls the contemporaneous advice of the apostle Paul to the Christian community at Corinth (I Corinthians 13). Telling the young church how to manage its practical affairs, he turned to a general word of advice, on how to follow 'the more excellent way' (the good way to which a man should cleave). He admonished the Christians to open their hearts:

> If ... I have not love, I gain nothing. Love is patient and kind, love bears all things, believes all things, hopes all things, endures all things ... so faith, hope, and love abide, these three, but the greatest of these is love.

This 'love' (*agape*) was a social virtue, an attitude toward men in community, not abstracted into 'humanity,' but love for each individual man who adhered to the unruly Christian community. The advice of the disciples of Yohanan, to seek the way of generosity, good companionship, broad vision (like faith, and hope) was subsumed likewise by Eleazar, in Yohanan's opinion, by his teaching on the good heart, which was the source of all abiding blessing and the beginning of virtue. Morality begins in the heart of man, with his effort to love not man but men; this was a specific, social virtue, and if Paul regarded love as the way to meet perplexities in the young church, Eleazar and his master Yohanan found the good heart no less central to the spiritual life of Jerusalem.

Thus a circle of students came together with Yohanan ben Zakkai for the study of moral questions. How did they happen to meet? At least two of them began their education with him, starting from the most elementary duties of religious life. One of these, Simeon ben Natanel, was apparently an ignorant man at the beginning, coming in his mature years from an unlettered family, and therefore Yohanan called him an 'oasis in the desert.'[18] The coming of the second, Eliezer ben Hyrcanus, was also at a mature age. It happened this way, according to one recension:

What were the beginnings of Rabbi Eliezer ben Hyrcanus? He was twenty-two years old, and had not yet studied Torah. One time he resolved, I will go and study Torah with Rabbi Yohanan ben Zakkai. His father Hyrcanus said to him, Not a taste of food shalt thou get before thou hast ploughed the entire field. He rose early in the morning, ploughed the entire field, and then departed for Jerusalem. It is told that the day was the evening of the Sabbath, and some say he went for the Sabbath meal to his father-in-law's, but some say, he tasted nothing from six hours before the eve of the Sabbath until six hours after the departure of the Sabbath. As he was walking along the road, he saw a stone. He picked it up and put it into his mouth. Some say, it was cattle dung. He went to spend the night at a hostel. Then he went and appeared before Rabban Yohanan ben Zakkai in Jerusalem, until a bad breath rose from his mouth. Said Rabban Yohanan ben Zakkai to him, Eliezer my son, hast thou eaten at all today? Silence. Rabban Yohanan ben Zakkai asked him again. Silence again. Rabban Yohanan ben Zakkai sent for the owners of his hostel and asked them, Did Eliezer have anything to eat at your place? We thought, he was very likely eating with you. He said, And I thought he was very likely eating with you. You and I, between us, left Rabbi Eliezer to perish. Thereupon Rabban Yohanan said to him, Even as a bad breath rose from thy mouth, so shall fame of thee travel for thy mastery of the Torah. When Hyrcanus his father heard of him, that he was studying Torah with Rabban Yohanan ben Zakkai, he declared, I shall go and ban my son Eliezer from my possessions. It is told, that day Rabban Yohanan ben Zakkai sat expounding in Jerusalem, and all the great ones of Israel sat before him. When he heard that Hyrcanus was coming, he appointed guards and said to them, If Hyrcanus comes, do not let him sit down. When Hyrcanus arrived, and they would not let him sit down, he pushed on ahead until he reached the place near Ben Ṣiṣit HaKeset, Nakdimon ben Gurion, and Ben Kalba Sabua [leading citizens in Jerusalem]. He sat down among them and trembled. It is told, On that day, Rabban Yohanan ben Zakkai fixed his gaze upon Rabbi Eliezer and said to him, Deliver the exposition. I am unable to speak, Rabbi Eliezer pleaded. Rabban Yohanan pressed him to do it, and the disciples pressed him to do it, so he arose and delivered a discourse upon things which no ear had ever before heard. As the words came from his mouth, Rabban Yohanan ben Zakkai rose to his feet, and kissed him upon the head and exclaimed, Rabbi Eliezer, master, thou hast taught me the truth. Before the time had come to recess, Hyrcanus his father rose to his feet and declared, My masters, I came here only in order to ban my son Eliezer from my possessions. Now all my possessions shall be given to Eliezer my son, and all his brothers are herewith disinherited, and have naught of them.[19]

A second source adds:

He said to him, If I were to seek from the Omnipresent silver and gold he would have what to give me, as it is said, Mine are the silver and gold (Haggai 2:8), and if I wanted land, he could give me, as it is said (Psalm 24:1) The earth is the Lord's, and the fulness thereof. I sought only, that I might find merit in Torah, as it is said (Ps. 119:118), Thou dost spurn all who go astray from thy statutes, yea, their cunning is in vain, all the wicked of the earth does thus count as dross; therefore I love thy testimonies, my flesh trembles for fear of thee, and I am in awe of thy judgments.[20]

Eliezer kept the promise of his youth, and became one of the great masters of the next generation. He married the sister of Gamaliel II. A loyal and devoted disciple of Yohanan, he escaped with him from Jerusalem and accompanied him to Yavneh. After Yohanan died, Eliezer left for Lud (Lydda) where he conducted his own court and academy.

He was devoted to tradition, and deeply conservative in his judicial philosophy. He was finally excommunicated for his stubbornness in holding to ancient traditions, and died in retirement, after a melancholy old age. When he died, the words of Yohanan ben Zakkai were on his lips.[21] He left three sayings:

> Let the honour of thy fellow be as dear to thee as thine own.
> Be not easily angered.
> Repent one day before thy death.

> Let the honour of thy fellow be as dear to thee as thine own: how so? This teaches that even as one looks out for his own honour, so should he look out for the honour of his fellow. And even as no man wishes that his own honour be made light of, so should he wish that the honour of his fellow shall not be made light of.

Eliezer's disciples asked him:

> Does a man then know on what day he will die, that he should know when to repent?

He replied:

> All the more so: let him repent today lest he die on the morrow. Let him repent on the morrow, lest he die the day after, and thus all his days will be spent in repentance.

His unhappy years of excommunication probably were reflected in the warning:

> Keep warm at the fire of the sages, but beware of their glowing coals lest thou be scorched, for their bite is the bite of the jackal, and their sting the sting of a scorpion. Moreover, all their words are like coals of fire.[22]

In later years, Eliezer's chief rival in the academy at Yavneh was Joshua ben Hananiah, Yohanan's earlier student at Jerusalem and prefect of his school. He left three sayings as well:

Avarice, an evil impulse, and hatred of mankind put a man out of the world. What is to be understood by avarice? This teaches that even as a man looks out for his own home, so should he look out for the home of his fellow, and even as no man wishes that his own wife and children be held in ill-repute, so should no man wish that his fellow's wife and children be held in ill-repute. There was once a certain man who begrudged his companion his learning, and his life was cut short and he passed away.[23]

The third student, Eleazar ben Arakh, said:

Be diligent in the study of Torah, and know how to answer an unbeliever.
Let not one word of the Torah escape thee.
Know in whose presence thou art toiling, and who is the author of the covenant with thee.[24]

Eleazar distinguished himself in mystical speculation, which he probably learned from Yohanan ben Zakkai.[25] After Yohanan died, he went to Emmaus, a mountain town which enjoyed a healthy climate, rather than to Yavneh, where his fellow students settled, and later lamented:

Settle in a place where the Torah is studied, and think not that it will seek thee, for only thy colleagues will perpetuate it in thy possession, and rely not on thine own understanding.[26]

He left almost no legal doctrines, having been out of touch with the main discussions of his mature years. He was a distinguished student who never kept the promise of his youth. He left the saying:

I am not a prophet nor the son of a prophet, but my teachers have taught me the ancient truth that every counsel enhancing the glory of God leads to good results.[27]

The fourth member of the circle was Yosi the Priest, surnamed 'the pious.' He said:

Let thy fellow's property be as dear to thee as thine own, make thyself fit for the study of Torah, for it will not be thine by inheritance, and let all thine actions be for the sake of heaven.[28]

Also involved in mystical speculation, he left very few teachings, and only one of a moral nature:

Beluriah the convert asked Rabban Gamaliel, It is written in your Torah, 'Who will not show favour' (Deut. 10:17), and it is written 'May God show you favour' (Num. 6:26). Rabbi Yosi the Priest engaged her. He said to her, I shall tell you a parable, to what is the matter compared? To a man who lent his fellow a coin, and arranged the time for repayment before the king, and the borrower swore to him by the life of the king. When the time came, he did not repay him. He came to appease the king, and the king replied, My claim is forgiven to you, but go and appease your fellow. Here also, scripture speaks of sins between man and God, and there, between man and man.[29]

The fifth member of the circle, Simeon ben Natanel, said:

Be prompt in reciting the Shema and the Prayer. When thou prayest, do not make thy prayer a routine, but a supplication before the Holy One, blessed be He, for it is said, 'For he is a God compassionate and gracious, long-suffering and abundant in mercy, and repenteth him of the evil' (Joel 2:13); and be not wicked in thine own sight.[30]

The five disciples[31] of Yohanan ben Zakkai reflected the main concerns of their academy. They sought to find ways to receive the divine words ('Qualify thyself for the study of Torah, since the knowledge of it is not an inheritance of thine ...'), to apply them to commonplace matters ('Let thy friend's honour be as dear to thee as thine own ...'), as well as to the broader issues of morality ('Repent one day before thy death ...') and to abstract from them fundamental principles for the conduct of the good life ('A good heart'). Strikingly, Eliezer, Joshua, and Yosi all repeat the reciprocal rule of good conduct laid down in Leviticus 19:18, 'Thou shalt love thy neighbour as thyself,' phrasing the law in more specific terms (honour, property, reputation). Thus they tried to bring the word to bear on day-to-day issues of life, and to create a society capable of accepting and embodying the divine imperative.

NOTES AND REFERENCES

[1] My LIFE OF RABBAN YOHANAN BEN ZAKKAI provides a full discussion of the relevant sources on his life and thought. Here it suffices to note the following: Yohanan ben Zakkai was a leading authority in the Pharisaic party before the destruction of the Temple in 70 C.E., and was instrumental in reconstituting it afterward, founding an academy at Yavneh (Jamnia) shortly before the destruction. He lived probably in Jerusalem, and, for a time, in a Galilean village. In the Galilee he was lonely, unimpressed by the charismatic wonder-workers he found there, but on his return to Jerusalem, he found the routine of cultic sacrifice equally unsatisfactory. While he venerated the Temple cult, he disliked the priests for their rejection of the Pharisaic claim to direct the cultic ceremonies. The Pharisaic alternative to charismatic faith on the one hand and cultic routine on the other was found in the study of the Torah (Hebrew Scriptures) which provided the Pharisaic sages with both a discipline and a pneumatic spiritual experience through study, interpretation, and application of Scripture. Yohanan's scriptural exegesis followed Hillelite principles, emphasizing the content of Scripture rather than linguistic or philological elements. He and his students investigated the mysteries of Ezekiel's vision of the divine Chariot (Ez. 1.8), probably as a means of achieving theosophical understanding. When the revolution of 66-73 C.E. broke out, Yohanan advised that the war was hopeless, and urged submission to imperial authority. When his advice was ignored, he and his students escaped from the city, allegedly by a ruse, and went to Yavneh, where they continued their learning. After the destruction, Yohanan comforted the people by teaching that if they would do the will of God, they might achieve redemption through their own moral regeneration. He gave renewed emphasis to the redemptive significance of acts of lovingkindness, even in place of Temple sacrifice, thus focusing on the means of service to God still available to Israel, namely, moral action guided by revealed law.

[2] Avot 1.15. Cf. ARNa, ch. 14, Schechter ed. p. 29a; Goldin tr. p. 74.

[3] Bereshit Rabbah 1.1. Cf. E. Goodenough, By Light, Light, The Mystic Gospel of Hellenistic Judaism (New Haven, 1935), 72-74; H. A. Wolfson, Philo (Cambridge, 1948), I, 242-3, 268; N. N. Glatzer,

Hillel The Elder: The Emergence of Classical Judaism (New York, 1956), 51-53; also my article, 'Does Torah Mean Law?' Journal of the Central Conference of American Rabbis, October, 1959, 42-45; Ebner, Elementary Education, 19-20. This conception of Torah/Wisdom was not unique to Hellenistic Judaism.

[4] Yohanan considered pursuit of wealth a hindrance to pursuit of Torah.

[5] Professor Morton Smith of Columbia University suggests the comparison to the *magus*, Cf. A. S. Schechter, 'A Glimpse of Social Life of the Jews in the Age of Jesus Son of Sirach,' Studies in Judaism: Second Series (Philadelphia, 1908), 55-101; W. O. E. Oesterly, The Books of the Apocrypha, their Origin, Teaching, and Contents (London, 1951), 326; C. C. Torrey, The Apocryphal Literature (New Haven, 1956), 95; R. Pfeiffer, History of New Testament Times with an Introduction to the Apocrypha (New York, 1945), 361, 'No one can become a scribe without leisure.'

[6] M. Segal, Sefer Ben Sira HaShalem (Jerusalem, 1959), 252. Segal's Hebrew text reads: If he will stand (endure), he will be more blessed than a thousand And if he rests, he will suffice (or leave) for himself a name.

[7] Segal comments (260), that if the scribe-sage lives long, he will leave a great name after death, and if he dies young, he will suffice with a good name.

[8] I think that the major particularity of the sages' society was their concern not for sacramental meals but for study of Torah.

[9] Cf. also I. Levi, La Légende de Pythagore de Grèce en Palestine (Paris, 1927); M. Hadas, Hellenistic Culture (New York, 1960), 194, 308 n. 20-23, 25; H. A. Wolfson, Philosophy of the Church Fathers (Cambridge, 1956), 1-3.

[10] S. Dill, Roman Society from Nero to Marcus Aurelius (New York, 1957), 200 f. Cf. also Hadas, Culture, 245.

[11] Parallels between Stoic and Pharisaic teachings have been studied by A. Kaminka, 'Les Rapports entre le rabbiniame et la philosophie stoicienne,' REJ, LXXXII (1926), pp. 233-252. Cf. also Bergmann (no first name given), 'Die Stoische Philosophie und die juedische Froemmigkeit,' Hermann Cohen Festschrift (Berlin, 1912), 145-166. Bergmann notes the parallel between Seneca's, 'One ought not to say, I have lost a son, but rather, I have given back a son' to Yohanan's bereavement and Eleazar's comfort. Cf. especially pp. 163-165, the contrast between rabbinic and philosophical learning. Cf. also Josephus, Life, 2, where he says that the Pharisees 'have points of resemblance to that which the Greeks call the Stoic school.' The major points of resemblance seem to be: first, the creation of an 'academic' society, and second, the focus on moral concerns. Professor Judah Goldin's study of this question in reference to Yohanan ben Zakkai's academy will be printed in the H. A. Wolfson 'festschrift' in the near future.

[12] Dill, 293.
[13] Ibid., 299.

[14] Sifre Numbers 123 (Friedman ed. p. 41a). Compare Tosefta Para 4:7. Another such incident is reported in Tos. Oholot 16:8. Joshua is reported to have commented, 'He who learns and does not review is like a man who sows and does not harvest, and a person who studies Torah and forgets is like a woman who bears and buries...'

[15] TB Baba Batra 10a. (Trans. by M. Simon, The Babylonian Talmud: Seder Nezikin, London, 1952, III, 44-8.)

[16] ARNa ch. 14, ed. Schechter p. 29a, Tr. Goldin 74 f. Avot 2:8 f. Cf. Finkelstein, Mavo, 38-44. The antiquity of these sayings (probably the oldest record of Yohanan ben Zakkai) is proven by the high praise recorded for Eleazar ben Arakh. Since he was isolated from the rabbis at Yavneh, one must assume that this collection of *logia* was edited before his reputation for learning was lost, and, therefore, during Eleazar's lifetime, if not during Yohanan's. Cf. Finkelstein, Mavo, 60-61. The 'three-fold cord' may refer to Joshua's learning, piety, and wisdom (Kohelet 4:12). Indeed, in the light of this praise, one may understand Joshua's recommendation of the good companion, for the verse continues, 'If two lie together, they are warm, but how can one be warm alone?' And though a man might prevail against one who is alone, two will withstand him. A three-fold cord is not quickly broken. Cf. also A. Kaminka, 'Stoic Parallels,' 238, who cites Seneca's *damnorum omnium maximum est, si amicum perdidisse*. Finkelstein comments (44) that a good heart is better than a good impulse, because the impulse is dependent on the goodness of the heart. Cf. also Hoenig, Sanhedrin, 176-8. The praise of Joshua's mother in Avot 2:8 may refer to her bringing him as an infant to hear the words of Torah, TP Yevamot 1:6. Note especially the variant reading of Abba Shaul in ARNb, ed. Schechter, p. 30a, 'Abba Shaul said in the name of Rabbi Akiba, who said in his (Yohanan's) name,...' Finkelstein notes that the dispute on the place of Eliezer and Eleazar among the next generation indicates the antiquity of the source. Cf. also Albeck, Seder Nezikin (Tel Aviv, 1953), 495. If, as seems likely, Abba Shaul's statement was made at Yavneh, it would certainly not support Allon's hypothesis that Eleazar left Yohanan before his death. Two other possibilities are, first, that the denigration of Eliezer in Eleazar's favour represents the later opposition to Eliezer, after his excommunication; second, the saying of Abba Shaul might be based on an earlier opinion of Yohanan, before Eleazar left him and the praise of Eliezer might be Yohanan's reaction to Eleazar's disloyalty. Allon might certainly argue so. If, however, the clause, 'and even if Rabbi Eliezer... were with them' is Abba Shaul's and not an interpolation, and there is no reason to doubt this, then it seems likely to me that the statement of Abba Shaul comes after the original praise for Eliezer; thus contradicting Allon. Cf. also the comments, *ad loc.* of Bertinoro, who suggests that the greater praise for Eleazar was on account of his superior acumen (certainly the plain sense of the text). The extant sources do not indicate this, but only Eleazar's great capacity for mystical speculation.

[17] ARNa ch. 14, ed. Schechter p. 29a, Goldin 75 f. For the expression

'go forth and see,' cf. TB Berahot 19a. Compare also the statement of Judah the Prince, Avot 2.1, 'Which is the right course that a man should choose for himself? That which he feels to be honourable to himself and which also brings him honour from mankind.'

[18] Finkelstein, Mavo, 43-44; and appendix III, 243-244. Tos. Avodah Zara 3:10. But compare the opinion of L. Ginzberg, Perushim veHiddushim BaYerushalmi, III, 334, cited by Finkelstein, 243.

[19] ARNa ch. 6, Schechter p. 15b f., Goldin, 43 f. ARNb, ch. 13, Schechter, p. 15b-16a. Parallels are in Yalkut Shimoni on Gen. p. 72; Gen. R. Ch. 41:1, Pirke de Rabbi Eliezer, chs. 1-2. The apparent interpolation about his father-in-law (who was Simeon ben Gamaliel I, cf. TB Nedarim 20a and below) is very difficult to understand. According to the beginning paragraphs in PRE, he was unmarried when he came to Jerusalem; and it is unlikely that he was married to the daughter of the Pharisaic leader before he had studied at the academy at all.

[20] This paragraph is added from Pirke de Rabbi Eliezer, ch. 2. Cf. also Trans. G. Friedlander (London, 1916), 8. The PRE account provides variant details. See also ARNb, ch. 13, Schechter 17a, n. 39, and p. 16a, n. 55.

[21] Cf. ch. 9; TB Nedarim, 20a; Baba Meziah 59b, TP Moed Katan 1.

[22] Avot 2:10, Bereshit R. 52, Pesikta Rabbati 9b. For a brief discussion of Joshua's and Eliezer's later careers, B. Z. Bokser, Pharisaic Judaism in Transition (New York, 1935), and Joshua Podro, The Last Pharisee (London, 1959).

[23] Avot 2:16. ARNa ch. 16, Schechter p. 31b, Goldin 82.

[24] Avot 2:19, ARNa ch. 17, Schechter 33b, Goldin 90.

[25] See Bab. Talmud Hagigah 14b, and my Life of Rabban Yohanan ben Zakkai, pp. 96-103.

[26] ARNa ch. 17, cited above; Kohelet Raba 7.7, cf. also TB Shabbat 147b, Avot 4.14.

[27] Midrash Tehillim 1.3.

[28] ARNa ch. 17, Schechter 33a, Goldin 87. The commentary of ARNa is as follows: 'Let thy fellow's property be as dear to thee as thine own: How so? This teaches that even as one has regard for his own property, so should he have regard for his fellow's property; and even as no man wishes that his own property be held in ill repute, so should he wish that his fellow's property shall not be held in ill repute.' Note the parallel comments on the teachings of Eliezer ben Hyrcanus in this connection, ARNa, ch. 15, Goldin 78; and of Joshua ben Hananiah, ARNa ch. 16, Goldin 82. Cf. also Avot 2:17.

[29] ARNa ch. 17, Schechter 33b, Goldin 90. Also Jonah 4:2. Goldin comments 194, n. 13 that the verse in the text does not correspond exactly either to Joel 2:13 or to Jonah 4:2, and the copyist may have quoted from memory.

[30] Avot 2:18.

[31] Other references to the main disciples are as follows: Eleazar ben Arakh: TB Shabbat 147b, Eruvin 13b, Hagigah 14a, b, Hullin 106a; TP Demai 7.7, Hallah 3.1, Hagigah 2.1, Yevamot 2.1, 3.4, 4.7, 6.4;

Nedarim 10.6, Kiddushin 1.1; also Mishnah Demai 7.7, Tos. Terumot 5. Tos Nedarim 6: 'Rabbi Eliezer said to Rabbi Akiba, It is unfortunate for you, for if you were in the days of Rabbi Eleazar ben Arakh, he would have answered you ...' Thus Eleazar died before Eliezer. Yosi the Priest: TB Shabbat 19a, Taanit 13a, b; Hagigah 14b; Rosh Hashanah 15b, 17b; Ketuvot 26b, 27a; TP Ketuvot 2.9; Mishnah Eduyot 8.2; Simeon ben Natanel: TB Mishnah Avot only TP Hagigah 2.1, Tos. Avodah Zara 3.1. Cf. also Bacher, Agadot, I, i, 50-53; Bruell, Mavo 87-8; Frankel, Mishnah, 94-95; A. Hyman, Toldot Tannaim ve-Amoraim (London, 1920, three vols.) s. v.; S. Mendelsohn, 'Eleazar ben Arak,' JE, V, 96-97; I. Broyde, 'Jose HaKohen,' JE, VII, 243-4; J. Z. Lauterbach, 'Simeon b. Natanel,' JE, XI, 356. On Stoic parallels, see also S. Lieberman, 'How much Greek in Jewish Palestine', in Alexander Altmann, ed., 'Biblical and Other Studies' (Cambridge, 1963), pp. 123-141.

IV

AN AFTER-WORD

Jewish Fellowship Today

JEWISH COMMUNITIES ARE mostly no longer communities at all, but rather conglomerate social groups composed of isolated individuals. Thus, in a given city, the Jews may share certain common purposes. To the world-at-large indeed, the Jews might seem to be 'clannish,' for often one finds neighbourhoods which are mainly Jewish, and notes that large numbers of Jews prefer the company of other Jews (no matter how desiccated their Jewishness may be). Yet when one examines the typical Jewish community carefully, one finds that the areas of common purpose and unique social experience are limited. What in fact manifests the element of 'communion' among Jewish individuals in a given place, to demonstrate that there truly is community among them? One would note the common efforts in foreign and domestic philanthropy, public relations ('defense'), social service through hospitals and homes for the aged, and even common institutions for social life ('community centres') and education. Perhaps the structure of the Jewish community is impressive by contrast to that of other groups in American society; perhaps Jews are even over-organized.

The Jews are not, however, a community in the ways that once characterized the Kennesset Yisrael, the Jewish People living in a given town or village. What were these ways? One learns from any of a dozen first-class social studies of

AN AFTER-WORD

Jewish life in the past (Yaakov Katz, TRADITION AND CRISIS; Salo W. Baron, THE JEWISH COMMUNITY are two) what the Jewish People once enjoyed as a community. The elaborate communal structure in the U.S.A. provides a pale contrast. The Jew in a medieval town in Europe or the Moslem world (and this town would likely have survived to the early 19th century in Western Europe, and to 1940 in the East, and, perhaps, even to 1948-9 in the Arab part of the Moslem world) may have been alien to the land of his birth, but he was very much at home among the people of his faith. He enjoyed, therefore, a social security one can today hardly envision, much less appreciate. He was known to all men, and knew all men; he had his place and his hour, and if neither was particularly exalted, both assured him against the present sense of *anomie* and personal alienation. He belonged.

In his place, however humble, he had a living or protection, at least, against starvation; he had friendship; he had the security of a rich and complex web of human relationships, which placed him into relationship with everyone he might meet, even the stranger, even the enemy. His neighbour was his companion; he prayed with him, studied with him; shared with him the crises of life; buried him; wept for him. Community meant, therefore, one's own address in life and beyond death; it meant continuity, and it meant love, if by love one understands the effort to reach out from one self to another. The Jewish community was a representation of Kennesset Yisrael here and now, and manifested the social reality to which the Torah was given, at which the Prophets raged, and for which the Sages devised their moral and legal constitution based on revelation and prophecy. In this community, each man had his particular role to play, a role which, under the circumstances of Judaism, had significance in the historical and metaphysical drama of creation, revelation, and redemption.

The Jewish community was not alone in its débacle. All 'traditional' society underwent similar strain, as Oscar

Handlin describes the pattern in The Uprooted; and the advent of modernism – industrialization, urbanization, overpopulation, and perhaps bourgeoisification as well – represented the end of community for many men in many places. If one may characterize several centuries of social history in the West, and, apparently, the present social tendency in the East as well, one would conclude that most men outside primitive societies are facing the crisis of community and the advent, for good or not, of the radically isolated individual as the basic unit of society. Individuals together, however, do not create a community; they create a mass. Indeed, the very concept of the individual apparently is based on the antithetical concept of the mass, as the concept of community (or tribe, or village) is apparently antithetical to any smaller, or larger, social unit (except possibly the family).

Contrasting American Jewish communities with those that existed in other places, therefore, yields a pattern with only slight variations (mainly temporal) from those of other people on the continent of North America and, now, throughout the others as well. Western society moved from its focus on the community to that on the individual over a period of many centuries. In the hardly precise, but still useful categories of Western history, one can trace a gradually evolving pattern of individuation in the West from the time of the rise of the nation-state, through the Renaissance and Reformation, and into the eras of industrial revolution, secularism, liberalism, and only lately, totalitarianism. Today man stands alone against the state. For the Jew, on the other hand, the same pattern emerged in relatively few years, at the most (to date) three generations for the larger part of the American Jewish community, perhaps five for Western European Jewry (what remains of it), and two or even one for much of Israeli Jewry, as well as that in Eastern Europe and Soviet Russia. The Jews seem to have experienced their renaissance and reformation and nationalization and secularization and bourgeoisification and, for some

AN AFTER-WORD

'totalitarianization' in about a century; not gradually but suddenly, even brutally; and, for one-third of them, tragically.

It is no wonder, then, that the Jewish community seems desiccated and colorless by contrast to that of earlier centuries. It is no wonder, either, that most Jews do not even enjoy a community at all, most of the time and for most of their lives. Many, at least, have a rather limited experience of Jewish community: in part, ritual (and that part diminishes in importance for many), in part, ethnic. To return then to the so-called Jewish community of a given city today, one asks whether it is a true community, and concludes that, by comparison with what men once experienced as 'community,' it is not. In most places, it is rather a collection of communities, mostly very very small, of cliques and clans and minuscule sibs; it is 'country clubs' for some, and community centres for some, and particular shops and synagogues and summer resorts for some. For none is the Jewish community co-extensive with all the Jews in a given place (as it was in New York City as late as 1800, and in Charleston, South Carolina, for still another quarter-century); for few is it a community at all. One would have to look very hard to find Kennesset Yisrael in a given place or time. The fundamental category of Jewish peoplehood has lost its referent in historical reality, and while it remains essential theology, it is poor sociology indeed. If one regards the past situation of Judaism as relevant and even authentic, however, one will recognize that the socially meaningful entity that was Kennesset Yisrael, that is, the Jewish people in a given place and time, needs in some measure to be restored and reconstituted. The relevance and authenticity of that earlier experience is this: to a particular people, revelation was handed down; to a particular society, the prophets gave their teachings; the artifacts of a particular social culture were the raw materials of the Rabbis. Judaism thus addressed itself to a community, not merely to 'individuals who share a common destiny'; that community represented the focus and embodiment of the Jewish faith. What we have today is, alas, all that remains of it.

One turns to analogues available in Jewish social history of an earlier day, to find a suggestion at least as to how men met such a crisis of community. Professor Morton Smith[1] demonstrated how the crisis of community was met by an earlier age. He shows that the twentieth century has no monopoly on 'modernism'; on the contrary, during the centuries after the conquest of Alexander (*ca.* 330 B.C.E.), the ancient Near East experienced a remarkable expansion of trade, population, industry. New governments, ruling new empires, effected the rationalization of commerce and the nurture of state capitalism; new men, not only adventurers from Hellas but Semites as well, brought new vigour and genius to the dormant economy and culture of the East. One consequence was the precipitous growth of great cities, and, more commonly, the founding of new cities on the foundations of ancient villages. Another was the acquisition of new values, which approved individual endeavour and ascribed positive merit to the achievements of this world. Still a third was the questioning of ancient beliefs and doctrines in the light of the new and successful ideas flowing in from Hellas; the old religions had to address themselves to a broader audience of believers and non-believers alike, in the speculative, abstract, and sophisticated language of Hellenic thought, instead of the mythic and primarily concrete discourse of earlier centuries. The crisis of community apparently was manifest, therefore, in the crisis of ancient culture, in the appearance of many men unbound by ancient bonds and ethics, and most important, in the creation of uprooted masses in cities. The primary social unit became the individual, in place of settled men in towns and villages where the primary social unit had been mainly the family and village or town itself, and in whose structure of relationships each man had found his place.

In the cities and among the masses of men, one discerns a very articulate response, through emergent, assertive individualism, to the new situation. In many places, some men separated themselves from the 'masses,' and in one way or another, formed social entities that provided community, a place and a definition for the individual. We have examined in some detail two such 'communities,' the first formed by close adherence to laws of tithing and ritual purity, and the second formed by the men who came together to study the Torah, and indicated parallel efforts. If the *haburah* was fundamentally a society for strict observance of laws of ritual cleanliness and holy offerings, and if the circle of master and disciples was fundamentally a 'study group,' still, both may represent social entities which have particular relevance to men who are not wholly satisfied with the community provided by social experience among undifferentiated masses and alienated, lonely individuals. To uncover points of relevance, one may usefully articulate the social policy apparently espoused by the fellowship. First, the fellowship represented a decision to find elements of community within the common society, rather than to create a community outside of it. Second, it took a critical view of society as it was, choosing to separate its members from it by keeping strictly to its primary ideal, and at the same time attempting to educate the common society in what it considered the right way. Third, the specific method of the fellowship was, first, to define its fundamental concerns, to determine on precisely what issues there would be absolutely no compromise; second, to provide an orderly way by which an individual from any part of society might come to hear and carry out these concerns, and to elaborate the rules which would guide the fellow in every possible situation he might meet, thus defining his relationship with outsiders and his specific obligations as a part of the fellowship. Finally, the purpose of the fellowship was extremely limited; it was in no sense a revolutionary sect, but rather a finite and tentative effort to achieve particular religious and social ends. The consequences may be discerned in the endurance of the ideal of the fellowship after the social disasters of 70 and 135 C.E., when the Pharisees successfully transformed the defeated nation into a national fellowship scattered throughout many lands and conditions.

If the crisis of community has its historical analogue, so too the ancient responses find modern parallel. Thus one may regard the revolutionary utopianism of the kibbutz movement as a modern form of Essenism, in which men separated themselves from the common society to build a new and better community. The kibbutz was meant, as Martin Buber described it in *Paths to Utopia*, to make possible the creation of a real community, in which each individual had his home, and 'all other inhabitants with whom he lives and works are all acknowledging and confirming his individual existence.' The kibbutz definition of a community was 'one in which every point of its being possesses potentially at least the whole character of community,' a place in which man might feel his own home'; it represented the effort to re-acquire 'in new tectonic forms, internal social relationships.' As a response to the crisis of community, the kibbutz was extraordinarily successful for some men, and quite irrelevant to most.

A second modern effort to transform the situation of the French Communitarian movement, is described by Erich Kahler in *The Tower and the Abyss*. Bringing together many different kinds of individuals, the communitarians created a rule, a community, neighbour groups, and a social entity (the community) which held in common the means of production, not as an effort to retire from the world but to remain in but not of it. Kahler holds that the communitarian groups, founded in 1940 in Valence, differ from other urban co-operatives in the focus of the communal effort: not primarily financial gain but rather the effort to restore the dignity of the individual in relationship to other individuals. The purpose of the communitarians was social, not economic gain. In striking ways, therefore, the communitarian movement apparently manifests similarity to the *haburah*.

When one considers the social life of American Jewry (and

perhaps other diaspora Jewish communities as well), he notes certain areas in which the idea of the fellowship may be relevant. The smallest coherent social unit of the present Jewish community is the synagogue (and its parallel, sometimes competing equivalents in organizational life, such as the Lodge or Chapter of one Jewish institution or another). If the synagogue was once co-extensive with the Jewish community, today it is not co-extensive even with the social life of its members. The synagogue in many places does not represent the embodiment in an institution of a community at all; it is neither the consequence nor the cause of community. It is rarely founded by men and women who themselves feel the need to give form to a pre-existent social experience; and it very often does not produce a coherent social experience for its members. It is many things to many men, but to few indeed does it represent the focus of a religious communal life.

What place, in truth, does the synagogue have in the social life of its members? For some few, it is the place where they sometimes go to pray; for some others, it is the instrument for the transmission of the rudiments of Judaism to the young (and that not very effectively); for others, it may provide the framework for certain recreational activities. In synagogues of more than a few dozen families, it is even possible for all members not to know one another, and in larger places, it is possible for the rabbi not to know each member of his 'flock.' Whatever the synagogue ought to be, it is very rarely a community or a religious fellowship. The various lodges and chapters and posts (their name is legion) usually consist of a small number of activists, and a long mailing list. They bring together a very few people, for a random moment in the month, and provide limited social experience (often recreative), but very little fellowship. Even in the more modest forms of synagogue and institutional life, such as the 'brotherhood' or 'sisterhood' or the youth group, one finds strangers meeting strangers, remaining strangers.

If one would want Jews to cluster about their synagogues, in small congeries of families, a solution might be possible for some. The synagogue might indeed constitute the focus for the social life of a given group, and, with its religious emphasis, might indeed represent the effort to constitute Kennesset Yisrael. One might even witness the formation of Essenic neighbourhoods in American cities, inhabited by families whose lives are turned inward on the life of their synagogue. They might, as men once did, live together, pray together, study together, and know one another in the subtle intimacies of daily life. In truth, such synagogues do exist in America, as some villages in Israel and elsewhere remain true representations of the ancient community.

For the most part, however, Jewish neighbourhoods develop not around synagogues, but vice versa. People who prefer to live 'with their own kind' are not motivated, for the most part, by a desire to maintain a common school and place of worship within an easy walk from home, or to have a common *sukkah* at *Sukkot* and a common *mikveh* and a common *minyan*. I am not sure what they seek among 'their own kind,' but I suspect that it is a social benefit denied them elsewhere: the right to be received not as a type ('the Jew') but as an individual. Among one's own kind, the Jew is not, in fact, a member of a minority any longer, or possibly of any socially differentiable group, but he achieves the radical individuation denied him by extenuating circumstances elsewhere. The neighbourhood ghetto would seem to have become, therefore, the instrument of achieving its very opposite: a place in the undifferentiated mass.

Perhaps a way of achieving community is indicated by the ancient fellowship. If men remain in the life of the city, they may still have some of the benefits achieved by those who abandon it, by delineating particular areas of meaningful observance, or ritual, or intellectual concern, the participation in which will designate a man part of an otherwise unarticulated group. The fellow did so, as we have seen, by choosing certain ritual laws which he believed to be fundamental, and by observing them under all circumstances; the result was that some men in the larger society recognized one another as a part of the same polity, and were able, for example, to eat with one another, secure in the knowledge that their meal was ritually undefiled and properly prepared according to the rules of agricultural tithes and heave-offerings. The fellowship was not made up of men who lived in the same neighbourhood or had frequent social relationships with one another; and yet it sustained itself, and apparently provided a useful social relationship for its members.

One might well ask how a contemporary fellowship would differ from other such social instruments to create community, such as fraternities or Masonic groups or luncheon 'service' societies. Formally it does not differ at all. Like the Mason, the fellow may live anywhere in a given town, undifferentiated from others; like him, his fellowship may be unobtrusive. The way of the ancient fellowship is, therefore, not unexplored by others. What will render it useful and unique to Jews is how they choose to articulate it. Several principles may guide thought on contemporary efforts to recover the experience of fellowship.

First, a meaningful social group among Jews ought to take its particular character and definition from the Jewish faith and tradition. It ought to be defined and formulated in terms consequential to the religion of Israel, representing the sociological effect of the religious phenomenon itself. A Jewish social group or fellowship ought to bear witness to an intrinsic sociological idea within Judaism. Is there such an idea? Professor Petuchowski's[2] proposes that there is; the idea is that the constitution of a people of Israel, in a given place and time, finds significance in the history and destiny of the Jewish people, its definitions in the faith and *mitzvot maasiot* of the Jewish people, its programme in the Torah of the Jewish people, in the fulfilment of the ethical and moral principles of the Jewish people, and in the dedication of the private person to the communal enterprise of the

Jewish people. If the Jewish people came into being at Sinai, then the constitution must be the Torah, the laws, those of the Torah; indeed, the very possibility of receiving the Torah was and is predicated upon the creation of such a sacred community, worthy of bearing witness to its precepts and of realizing them in its community life. So Professor Petuchowski states:

> 'The Jew in the past approached his God as a member of the chosen people. He performed his Jewish obligations because they added the dimension of sanctity, which is the "constitution" of this chosen people ... When the Jew in the past submitted to the regimen of Torah-law, it was not so much a case of his being personally committed to this or that aspect of it, but simply of his being a member of a people which had committed itself to the Torah as its constitution.'

The *haburah* represents the effort to achieve much more than friendship or companionship, the effort to overcome personal loneliness. Rather, its purpose is fellowship, a very different experience. What distinction stands between fellowship and friendship? Friendship involves two people – fellowship, two people and one ideal held in common. Friendship is the consequence of primarily interpersonal and reciprocal benefit, sometimes intellectual, sometimes emotional, sometimes psychological. Friends need each other, otherwise they cannot remain friends. It is a static relationship. Friendship rests on abiding affection, it is entirely a cathectic relationship of two people, totally focused on those two people. Fellowship, on the other hand, may very well be achieved without friendship at all, for it is predicated on a common goal or ideal shared among two or more people, drawing them together despite, not because of, their particularities and uniquenesses.

In this sense, friendship is irrelevant to fellowship. One cannot doubt that out of genuine fellowship, friendship arises, but that is a happy by-product of a quite different experience. Fellowship engages isolated individuals in a common enterprise, thereby creating between them common bonds, providing for them common experience, uniting them for reasons quite external to the structure of their own personalities. This distinction is recognized in Avot:

> 'Whenever love depends upon some thing, with the passing away of that thing, the love too passes away; but if it be not dependent upon such a thing, it will not pass away forever.'

Fellowship, in an affirmative sense, depends upon a quality external to the relationships of those who are fellows of one another; it is that which unites two men who walk together down a path. When they reach their goal, they go their separate ways. To the extent that the fellowship imposes a common bond of purpose and direction upon men, it will differ from all activities intended to 'bring people together' or to facilitate personal needs of its communicants, to that extent it will not be another clique or club or clan. The ideal of fellowship thus exhibits a certain austerity uncommon in the effusive personal relationships we know and expect, for it is an ideal of men's coming together for utterly impersonal – in this sense, social – purposes. Friendships never transcend individual friends; fellowship must begin with such transcendence.

Third, the fellowship is to be created by the very personal involvement of each man in the ultimate purpose of the fellowship itself, in activities directly and immediately relevant to its final goal. Most organizational life professes an impressive galaxy of purposes; if only partly successful, any single American Jewish society would already have 'saved' the Jews, if not the world. The role of individuals in such organizations has very little to do with those ultimate purposes, however.

What, indeed, does the private person do in any society, including the synagogue? Mainly, the private person seems to give money and drink tea. For example, the great Jewish organizations in this country carry out enormously important tasks in philanthropic and Zionist activity, or in defence, or in education. But what do the members do? They pay dues, contribute to special 'drives' or 'campaigns,' receive 'bulletins' or communiqués, and very occasionally attend a meeting? (The very military character of organizational metaphors is appropriate indeed to the status of the private in the ranks, contented to do his duty, and sometimes, to get a medal – or a plaque.) What happens at a meeting? Generally, the members hear a speaker, perhaps ask a question, but mainly look forward to the coffee hour afterwards. This is quite legitimate, it seems to me, for the coffee hour is the one moment in which each private person actually does something creative and personal. The purposes of the organization are generally carried out by professionals. No matter the 'cause,' most men and women who support it have very little to do themselves towards achieving it.

For 'fellowship,' it ought to be contrary. The individual member ought to participate at every recreative moment in contributing not to the means of the group, but to its ends. He ought to contribute himself to reach such ends, and I mean himself, and not his money. If the fellowship begins with a budget it will end with a bank-account. Its goals must be so chosen that they may immediately engage each member. If each man knows and accepts the goal of the fellowship, and knows how he himself is achieving that goal personally, in his own being, then he will be more than a Lion or an Elk or a Benevolent Moose: he will be a Jew and a man.

Every activity in Jewish life, even the synagogue, permits its participants to fulfil their obligations by a money-payment, a kind of ransom for the absent soul. The cash nexus, however, represents the reduction of men to things. Money is easier to collect than minds. Intellect and commitment are more precious because they are rarer. In planning the *haburot*, one may profitably eliminate, so far as possible, the things of this world in pursuit of the blessings of the next.

AN AFTER-WORD

Finally, one ought to recognize, as did the ancient *haber* and *Talmid Hakham*, the very temporal character of fellowship or 'community' itself. Fellowship has no substance. It is not a social continuum. It manifests no existence independent from that of its communicants. Fellowship is a dimension of time: one cannot say fellowship is, but rather, fellowship happens. It is created and re-created from moment to moment when certain elements, namely, radically isolated individuals, coalesce to create it. The catalyst of fellowship needs to be discovered and defined. The components of fellowship are individuals coming together out of radical self-involvement and isolation from one another, to pursue a purpose that transcends their own individual lives.

There is, moreover, an element of recurrence in fellowship, an element of temporal return: day by day and moment by moment, fellowship is re-created. In this sense, there is a mythic quality to the ideal of fellowship. Myth attempts to represent underlying, recurring realities, that may be 'essences' of being, but are realized here and now only in their particularities. In this sense, again, there is a mystery to the realization of fellowship, and its very intangibility hints at this. Fellowship is the miracle that occurs when men and women transcend themselves, their personal wants, and subjective needs, in pursuit of an end, however petty, that lies beyond the horizons of their private place in life.

The fellowship in ancient times rested on the ideal of commonwealth, the sense that some men actually had common concerns and commitments which might be articulated through that particular institution. If there is in the end no underlying community in which men actually participate and for which they care, the fellowship is a useless device. From this viewpoint, however, one finds some slender hope: the Jews do seem to choose to remain a group, as the existence of Jewish neighbourhoods, hotels, fraternities, and the synagogues themselves testify. If this choice is a negative one, its consequences do not have to be negative. One can attempt to transform a group which finds its definition by contrast to the 'outside world' into a group which is constituted on affirmative inward social experience. Even today the Jews continue to manifest certain qualities of a fellowship; if not in a given synagogue, then in a given town, they do acknowledge their fellowship in some ways. One might well criticize the expressions of that fellowship, but one cannot ignore its presence in American cities. Attenuated ties bind Jews into an attenuated community. On this basis one may hope to recover the reality of fellowship and community.

Fellowship will not save the world, nor probably even make much of a difference to the Jewish community. It may matter, however, to the mundane life of the private person who controls very little more than how he spends his own time. I believe it may provide some men and women with a worthier 'cause' than that which now informs their lives. It is an interim programme, intended to meet very humble problems of social and personal conduct by directing the attention of perplexed men to higher purposes that they may achieve together. If it has any value at all the fellowship must be regarded as a tentative and austere step towards meaningful and creative use of that interim between birth and death that each man knows as life.

REFERENCES

[1] Morton Smith, Judaism in Palestine, I: To the Maccabean Revolt (at present in the Harvard Archives).

[2] Jakob Petuchowski, 'Toward a Modern "Brotherhood"' [The Reconstructionist, Dec. 16, 1960]. See also my 'Fellowship in Judaism,' Judaism, spring 1963, for further discussion of the theory and practice of Jewish religious fellowship today.

INDEX

Passages cited

I Hebrew Scriptures
Leviticus, *19.18* 55
Jeremiah, *2.2* 12
 3.14 29
Joel, *2.13* 54
Jonah, *4.2* 58
Kohelet, *4.12* 57

II New Testament
Matthew, *10.34–7* 17
I Corinthians, *13.1 f.* 49

III Talmudic and Midrashic Passages
Mishnah
 Berakot, ch. *8* 36
 Demai, ch. *2* 24–6, 36–8
 Sotah, ch. *9* 29
 Avodah Zarah, ch. *4* 35
 Eduyot, ch. *5* 20
 Avot, ch. *1* 21, 41
  ch. *2* 52–4
  ch. *5* 71
 Hullin, ch. *2* 36
 Bekerot, ch. *3* 37
 Kelim, ch. *17* 37
Oholot, ch. *18* 37
Makshirin, ch. *1* 37
Tosefta
 Demai, ch. *2* 25–6, 36–40
 Shabbat, ch. *1* 29
 Makshirin, ch. *3* 35–6
 Kelim, ch. *7* 37
 Taharot, ch. *5* 37
Babylonian Talmud
 Sotah, *48a* 35
 Baba Metsiah, *87a* 36
 Baba Bathra, *10a*, 46
 Nazir, *46b* 37
 Bekorot, *30a/b* 29, 36–8
Palestinian Talmud
 Berakot, ch. *9* 36
 Demai, ch. *2* 36
 Sotah, ch. *5* 36
Midrashim
 Sifre Numbers, *para. 123* 46
 Avot de R. Nathan, ch. *6* 49–51
  ch. *14* 47–8
  ch. *15* 58
 Bereshit Rabbah, ch. *1* 42
  ch. *44* 36
 Midrash Tehilim, ch. *7* 36
 Pirke de R. Eliezer, chs. *1–2* 49–51

General Index

Abba Shaul, 36, 38, 47, 57
Abraham, 16, 36
Academic philosophers, 44
Akabya ben Mahaleleel, 20
Akiba, R., 58–9
Albeck, C., 35, 57
Allon, G., 35–6, 38, 57
Am Ha-Aretz, 14, 22–4
Anomie, 61

Bacher, W., 59
Baron, S. W., 61
Baumgarten, J., 34
Ben Sira, cited, 42–3
Bokser, B. Z., 58
Brandt, W., 35
Broyde, I., 59
Bruell, N., 59
Buber, M., 66
Buechler, A., 34–5

Charleston, S. C., 63
Christian Community (Nazarenes), 44, 49
Corinth, 49
Communitarians, 66

Demai, laws concerning, 23–36
Dill, S., 56

Eleazar b. Arakh, R., 47–57
Eliezer b. Hyrcanus, R., 47–57
Emmaus, 53, 59
Epstein, J. N., 38
Essenes, 13, 15–16, 35, 39

Fellow, fellowship—see *Haber, haburah*
Finkelstein, L., 36, 37, 38, 57–8
Frankel, Z., 59
Friendship vs. Fellowship, 73–4

Gamaliel I, 43
Gamaliel II, 51–54
Garments, 26, 37, 46
Gaster, Theodore, 21
Geiger, A., 40
Ghetto-neighbourhoods, 68–70, 73
Ginzberg, L., 39
Glatzer, N. N., 55–6
Goldin, J., 55, 56, 58
Goodenough, E., 55

Haber, Haburah, 11–21, 22–34, 44, 65–70, 72–3

General Index

Haburah shel Mitzvah, 40
Hadas, M., 56
Handlin, O., 61-2
Harrison, J., 35
Heave-offerings, 14-21, 22-34
Hillel, 16, 21, 25-7, 33, 46
Hoenig, S., 57
Hulin—see secular produce
Hyman, A., 58-9

Jerusalem, 12, 13, 41, 43, 44, 47, 49, 51
Jonah, R., 25-6
Josephus, cited, 14, 15, 16, 35, 43, 56
Joshua ben Hananiah, R., 47-56
Judah, R., 28-9, 38
Judah b. R. Shalom, R., 46
Judah the Prince, R., 58

Kahler, E., 66
Kaminka, A., 56-7
Katz, Y., 61
Kennesset Yisrael, 60-1, 63, 68
Kibbutz, 69

Lauterbach, J. Z., 59
Law, social function of, 19-20, 29-30
Levi, I., 56
Levites, 23, 27, 33-4
Lieberman, S., 21, 25, 35-8
Liquids, 26, 37
Lud (Lydda), 51

Maddaf-uncleanness, 39
Manual of Discipline, cited, 12, 19, 20, 21
Meir, R., 28-9, 32
Mendelsohn, S., 59
Midrash-uncleanness, 39
Moses b. Maimon, 36-8

Nabataeans, 15
Newcomer to fellowship—see novice
New York City, 63
Nilsson, M., 35
Novice, novitiate, 23-34

Oaths, 17, 36
Oesterly, W., 56

Paul, 49
Pedagogy, 46-7
Peripatetic Philosophers, 44
Petuchowski, J. J., 69-70, 74
Pfeiffer, R., 56

Pharisees, 13-21, 22-34, 38-9, 41-56
Philanthropy, 60, 71-2
Philo, cited, 13, 21, 35-6
Podro, J., 58
Priests, 22-3, 27, 33-4
Purity laws—see ritual purity, laws of
Pythagoreans, 15, 56

Qumran Community, 11-21, 44

Rabin, C., 36, 38, 40
Rashi, 36-8
Reliability, status of, 23-34
Ritual defilement, 22
Ritual purity, laws of, 14-21, 22-34, 37-9, 65-6
Rome, 45-6

Sadducees, 38-9
Schechter, S., 55-6
Schuerer, E., 38
Secular produce (*hulin*), 16, 22-34
Segal, M., 56
Seneca, 44-5, 56-7
Shamai, 16, 25-7, 33
Simeon b. Gamaliel, R., 43
Simeon b. Natanel, R., 47-56
Slaves, 17, 23, 31
Smith, M., 56, 64, 74
Synagogue, 66-68, 72, 74

Talmid Hakham, ideal of, 41-6, 73
Tax Farmer, 29
Terumah gedolah—see heave-offering
Thanksgiving Scroll, cited, 12-13
Tithes, laws of, 14-21, 22-34
Torah, study of, 41-56
Torrey, C. C., 56

Utopianism, 11, 15, 17, 18, 20

Valence, 66

Washing hands, 16
Wings, 25-7, 37
Wolfson, H. A., 55, 56

Yavneh, 51-3, 55
Yohanan ben Zakkai, 41-56
Yosi the Priest, 47-56

Zadokite Community, 15, 19
Zadokite Fragments, cited, 15, 19, 21
Zeitlin, S., 39